RABBIT CARE

HOW TO CARE FOR A RABBIT

D. J. EVA

Copyright © 2013

Disclaimer: The information contained in this book is for reference only and is not intended in any way as a substitute for professional veterinary medical advice. You must seek veterinary advice prior to commencing any rabbit care advice in this book.

CONTENTS

CHAPTER 1
HISTORY OF THE DOMESTIC RABBIT

The earliest evidence of rabbits dates to 10 million years ago in Europe and rabbits have been an important part of human life since the Middle Paleolithic period 30,000 years ago.[3,6]

Humans hunted rabbits and depended on them for meat and fur.[6] Our bond with these creatures became stronger when medieval monks domesticated them as farm animals. The first mention in literature of specific characteristics of domestic rabbits, such as size and color, were noted by Agricola, an Italian monk in the 16th century.[2]

By the mid-1800s, breeds such as the Himalayan, Angora and Silvers were being mentioned in English trade and livestock show literature.[2] Domestic rabbits became more popular as house pets or "house rabbits" in the mid-1800s, and the first Lop Club was formed in the 1840s in Europe.[2] Though today rabbit remains a food source in many parts of the world, house rabbits are extremely popular in Western countries and are the third most popular pet in British households.[5]

The American Rabbit Breeders Association, the House Rabbit Society and the British Rabbit Council are examples of current organizations that support and promote the breeding and welfare of domestic rabbits.[1,4]

1.	About the ARBA. (n.d.). Retrieved June 3, 2013, from American Rabbit Breeders Association, Inc. website: https://www.arba.net/about.htm

2.	American Veterinary Medical Association. (2007). U.S. Pet Ownership & Demographics Sourcebook. Retrieved from https://ebusiness.avma.org/EBusiness50/files/productdownloads/sourcebook.pdf

3.	Interesting Rabbit Domestication History. (2005, September 1). Retrieved June 3, 2013, from The American Livestock Breeds Conservancy website: http://www.albc-usa.org/news/sept1a_05.html

4.	O'Meara, H. (n.d.). A Natural History of House Rabbits. Retrieved June 3, 2013, from House Rabbit Society website: http://www.rabbit.org/journal/4-1/HRJ4.1%20Behavior.html

5.	Mission Statement: Official Website of the British Rabbit Council. (2010). Retrieved June 3, 2013, from British Rabbit Council website: http://www.thebrc.org

6.	Royal Society for the Prevention of Cruelty to Animals (RSPCA) All About Animals: Rabbits. (n.d.) Retrieved June 3, 2013, from RSPCA website: http://www.rspca.org.uk/allaboutanimals/pets/rabbits

7.	Than, K. (2013, March 11). Failure to Hunt Rabbits Part of Neanderthals' Demise? Retrieved June 3, 2013, from National Geographic Daily News website: http://news.nationalgeographic.com/news/failure-to-hunt-rabbits-part-of-neanderthals--demise-/

CHAPTER 2
DOMESTIC RABBIT BREEDS

All domestic rabbits are descended from the wild European rabbit, *Oryctolagus cuniculus*. Descendants of these first domestic breeds are still being selected and cross-bred today and numerous breed clubs and rabbit fancier groups have been formed around the world. Domestic rabbits appeared in the New World after the 1840s and surprisingly, no domestic breeds have been developed from the many North American wild rabbit species.

The American Rabbit Breeders Association recognizes forty-seven unique rabbit breeds and many varieties can be found within these breeds. The British Rabbit Council recognizes eighty-one official rabbit breeds.[2,4] According to the British Rabbit Council, breeds are generally categorized into the following types: Fancy, Lop, Normal Fur and Rex.[4]

General personality characteristics have been outlined for the breeds included here, but keep in mind that each rabbit is an individual and may not act exactly like another of the same breed.[17] The basic colors described here are recognized by the British Rabbit Council.[4]

COLORS

Agouti Pattern
The Agouti Pattern overall is a red-sandy color edged with white with slate gray undercolor.[4] There are thin orange

and yellow streaks across the back and the ears are trimmed in black. The eye circles, under the tail and inside the ears are white. The eyes are brown and nails are brown or black. Other variations of the Agouti Pattern include the dark, rich red Belgian Hare, Blue-Gray, Brown-Gray, the orange-brown Castor, the silvery-gray Chinchilla, the dusty brown Cinnamon, the dark blue-black Flemish, the Gray, the fawn-wheat Lynx-Wheaten, the gray dusted fawn Opal, the light gray Perlfee, the Red Agouti-Deilenaar, Sandy, and the sparkling light silver-gray Squirrel.

Patterned Colors
Patterned colors are spotted or alternating color patches of two or more colors. Common patterned colors include:

Broken: White overall coat color with patches of a different color

Butterfly: White overall coat color with regular colored pattern. The shoulders and sides are usually white.

Dalmatian: White overall coat color with randomly placed colored spots.

Dutch: Overall colored coat with white saddle and face.

English: Overall white coat with a stream of spots from shoulder to hip. The head is white with a colored butterfly covering the top lip and nose with eye circles.

Hotot: Overall pure white coat all over with dark eye circles.

Papillon: Similar to the English pattern but with far fewer spots on the flanks.

Rhinelander: Overall white coat with black and orange

marks. There is a black and orange colored line down the back and a few black and orange flank spots. Ears are splotched orange and black and the legs are white.

Self-Colored
Self-colored coats include: Black, Blue, Blue eyed white, Chocolate brown, Havana, Ermine, Ivory, Lilac, Red Eyed White, and Smoke.

Shaded self-color patterns are generally one solid light color such as cream or white with darker colored "points" on the face, belly, ears, face and tail. Possibilities include Bronze, Bluepoint, Chocolate Tortoiseshell, Seal Point, Siamese Sable, Siamese Smoke, Sooty-fawn, and Tortoiseshell. Shaded Tan patterns include all shades of Marten Sable. These colors range from very light creamy brown top color with slate undercolor to medium brown and dark dusty black-brown top color. Marten smoke is a slate undercolor with pearl gray beige top color and shaded gray with a blue-gray sheen.

Silvered Colors
Silvered colors have a flashy silver-gray coat sheen and come in a variety of base colors. These include Argente bleu, brun, crème, champagne, noir, silver fawn, gray, brown, and blue. The Meissener silver color is an overall black-blue coat with a heavy sprinkling of white hairs throughout.

Other Colors
The Harequin color patterns are a patchwork of golden orange and a darker color, such as brown, black, blue or lilac.

The Magpie coloring is a patchwork of a dark color such as black, brown, blue or lilac and white, but the dark color is seen in stripes. One ear is the dark color and the other ear is white. Two legs are a dark color while the other two are white and the face is half of each color.

FANCY BREEDS

Angora

The Angora has a "snowball" or round "powder puff" appearance. Adults are no larger than 3.4kg (7.5 pounds) and have a broad short head and short tufted ears. Their hair or wool is silky and thickly covers the feet. Colors include golden, fawn, cream, sable, all shades of marten, chocolate, smoke, and blue. Agouti colors also occur, and these are seen as mixtures of two or more colors, such as brown-gray, brown-gray and cinnamon. Angoras are gentle, wise and have relaxed personalities.[10,18]

Dutch

The most notable feature of the Dutch rabbit breed is the "saddle" junction between white and colored fur on the back. This is a rounded, compact breed and the individual's shape can determine its type within the breed. Adults are about 2.25kg (4.5-5 pounds) in body weight and have short and strong ears that are broad at the base. Colors include black with dark hazel eyes, blue with dark blue eyes, chocolate with brown eyes, yellow with hazel eyes, tortoiseshell with hazel eyes, and steel, pale or brown-gray with hazel eyes. Dutch rabbits are good-natured, sociable, easily trained.[18]

Tri Color Dutch

The body type, size, personality and stature of the Tri Color Dutch rabbit are similar to the Dutch breed.[1,4,18] One cheek must be orange and the other black. The ear on the orange side must be black and the ear on the black side must be orange. Blue and chocolate colors instead of black are also seen.

Himalayan

The Himalayan is a slender breed with a short, fine and pure white coat accented by "points" or markings on the feet and legs. Adults weigh approximately 2 kg (4.4 pounds). Color points seen on the feet and legs are black, blue, chocolate or lilac. Himalayans typically have relaxed personalities.[18]

Polish
The Polish rabbit is a small, pure white fine-boned rabbit with blood red or deep blue eyes. The Polish has erect ears and adults weigh at most 1.13kg (2.5 pounds). They have a fine-haired coat that characteristically quickly flies back into its original position when the coat is stroked in reverse. Polish rabbits are curious, gentle and very intelligent.[18,19]

English
English adult rabbits are approximately 2.7-3.6kg (6-8 pounds) and have characteristic cheek spots, a butterfly smut on the face and circle around each eye. Judges consider cheek spots touching the eye circles to be a fault. Colors include black, blue, tortoiseshell, chocolate or gray. English rabbits are friendly, outgoing and playful.[11]

Flemish Giant
These large rabbits weigh no less than 4.9 for bucks and 5.4kg for does (11-12 pounds) and have a dark steel gray color. The hair on the face can be darker than the body hair, and "ticking" is seen on the feet. Flemish Giants have relaxed, calm personalities.[18]

Harlequin
The Harlequin breed can be mistaken for the Tri-Color Dutch due to similarities in coat color pattern. The Harlequin is larger than the Tri Color Dutch, adult weight ranging 2.7-3.6kg (6-8 pounds). The striking color pattern on the head is equally divided; one side black and the other

11

side golden orange. This alternating, divided pattern is also seen on the legs, for example, one front leg is orange, the opposite rear leg is black. Harlequin color combinations include black and golden orange, lavender blue and fawn, dark brown and golden orange, dove gray and golden fawn. If the darker colors are alternating with white instead of the golden orange or fawn, those rabbits are called "magpies." Harlequins have a gentle, relaxed personality.[18]

Giant Papillon
This breed is also known as the Checkered Giant.[7] A robust, broad rabbit with the well-defined characteristic "papillon" or butterfly pattern of the nose and rounded cheek spots below the eye circles. Adult size is more than 5 kg (11 pounds). The hair coat is thick and short. All colors are seen in this breed, but the base color is always white. They have a reputation for having excitable personalities.[18]

Belgian Hare
Belgian Hares closely resemble wild hares in their stature and appearance. Belgians are long, muscular rabbits with sloping erect ears and a short, stiff deep chestnut red coat. There are no "ticking" or markings found on the legs or feet. Adults range in weight between 3.6-4kg (8-9 pounds). They are very large hares, very energetic, intelligent and require a lot of space for movement.[3]

Tan Hare
The Tan Hare is a long, muscular tan and black rabbit with hazel eyes and a ring of tan around each eye. Adults weigh about 3.6-4kg (8-9 pounds) and no other colors are allowed in this breed.

Lionhead
The Lionhead is recognized by its luxurious mane extending from the head onto the chest. The breed is also short and stocky with relatively short ears (about 7.5cm in

length). Adults weigh over 1.7 kg (3.75 pounds). All colors are seen in this breed and eyes can be red, blue, hazel or brown. The Lionhead has been described as "attention craving", smart and very gentle in personality.[13]

Netherland Dwarf
This dwarf breed is compact and cobby with short legs. The ears are erect, well furred and rounded at the tips. Adults weigh around 0.9kg (2 pounds). All recognized colors are seen, such as orange, steel, sable, lilac, brown, white, black, blue, tortoiseshell or agouti patterned. These rabbits have the reputation of being gentle, curious but sometimes skittish.[14]

Rhinelander
A barrel-shaped, medium to large sized rabbit with adults weighing 2.75-4.5 kg (6-10 pounds). The hair is silky and the base color is white, with striking black and yellow markings in a mosaic-like pattern. Round cheek spots of both colors and a full butterfly marking on the head are noted. Rhinelanders can have excitable, energetic personalities.[18]

Silver
The Silver rabbit has a short, soft coat that is seen in several shades, including silver gray, fawn, brown, and blue. The coat accent of "silvering" is seen throughout the hair coat all over the body. Ideal weight for adults is 2.27-2.72kg (5-6 pounds). Silvers are generally considered to have excitable personalities.[18]

Tan
The Tan rabbit is short, stocky and is most commonly seen in the black and tan color. Variations of blue, chocolate or lilac and tan are also noted. They have a solid black head with a ring of tan around each eye. These rabbits can be distinguished from the Tan Hare not only

by their size but by the two tan spots, known as "Pea Spots" at the dorsal root of the ears. Adults weigh approximately 2kg (4.4 pounds). Tan rabbits typically have very curious personalities.[18]

Thrianta

The Thrianta is considered a Tan rabbit but is a brilliant orange color. The undercoat is a striking, intense orange or red undercoat. They have similar weight and body characteristics to the Tan. Thrianta rabbits are gentle, friendly and curious.[20]

Tri Color English

This tri-colored breed has a perfect butterfly smut on the head, no white on the ears and a herring-boned saddle. Color combinations are mixtures of white base color with black and orange or blue and yellow. Adult weight is 2.7-3.6kg (6-8 pounds). English rabbits are friendly, outgoing and playful.[11]

Black Hare

The Black Hare is a long, muscular, fine boned rabbit in a black color with erect ears. The coat should be devoid of white or brown-tinged markings. Adult weight is 3.6-4kg (8-9 pounds).

LOP BREEDS

Lop breeds are characterized by their floppy ears and are seen in dwarf and normal sizes, all colors and coat textures. The ears may be seen in many different lengths and commonly, long-eared flops have ears that touch the floor when they are sitting.[12] Many of the different Lop breeds are very similar to each other in personality, character and body conformation. The French Lop is the descendant of English Lops that were crossed with

Normandy and Flemish Giants.[15] Lops generally are curious, relaxed, sweet and enjoy human interaction.[15]

Cashmere Lop
The Cashmere Lop is a short-bodied rabbit and adults weigh about 2.38 kg (5.25 pounds). The ears are broad, thickly furred and have rounded ends. The position of their lopped ears gives their head a "horseshoe" shape. The coat is dense with a long topcoat and is seen in all colors including agouti patterns.

Miniature Cashmere Lop
This is a smaller version of the cashmere lop and they share ear and conformational qualities. Adults weigh a maximum of 1.60 kg (3.5 pounds).

Lop Dwarf
This is a stocky, compact and well-muscled dwarf rabbit with well-furred, rounded ears. The butterfly nose marking fully covers the top lip and nose. The hair is short in length and is seen in all colors. Adults weigh 1.93-2.38kg (4.2-5.2 pounds).

English Lop
The English lop is a thick bodied rabbit that has thick, leathery ears and is seen in a variety of colors. Their body is described as having a "mandolin" shape and adults weigh over 2.7 kg (10.5 pounds).

French Lop
The French Lops have massive, muscled body type and have little visible neck. They have broad, thick ears but unlike the English Lop, the ears are well-furred. The minimum weight for adults is 4.5kg (10 pounds) and they are seen in a variety of colors.

German Lop

The German Lop is well muscled, large and has little visible neck like the English and French Lops. However, they distinguished from other Lops by their "Roman nose" appearance and large cheeks. Adults are slightly smaller than other Lops, 2.95-3.85kg (6.5-8.5 pounds) and are seen in all colors.

Meissner Lop
Meissner Lops are large and stocky with an arched facial profile. Meissner Lops are not as stocky as the French Lop. All self-colors and yellow are seen with silvering evenly over the entire body. Maximum weight of adults is 5.5kg (12 pounds).

Miniature Lop
Miniature Lops are stocky, small and with little visible neck. Miniature Lops are not a dwarf breed. Ears are broad, thick, rounded at the ends and well furred. Despite their smaller body size, the term "miniature" in their name refers to the size of the ear, not the size of the rabbit.[12] Miniature Lops are seen in chocolate tortoiseshell color, with an orange top color and brown along the ears, belly and under the tail and brown eyes. Maximum adult weight is 1.6 kg (3.8 pounds). Mini Lops are generally gentle rabbits in temperament.[18]

NORMAL FUR BREEDS

Alaska
Despite its name, the Alaska rabbit originated in Germany. Alaska rabbits, were developed for fur production, but are more popular today as pets and show animals.[21] Alaska rabbits are stocky with broad, well furred erect ears. They are blue-black in color, with an intense black covering most of the body. The undercolor is a deep slate blue. Adults weigh 3.17-4.08kg (7-9 pounds). They have an

even-tempered, gentle personality.[21]

Argente Bleu, Brun, Crème
Argente breed rabbits are stocky, compact and have a short neck. Their ears are short, fine-boned, rounded and erect. Adult weight is approximately 2.72kg (6 pounds). The Bleu, Brun, Crème, Noir and Champagne are each separate breeds according to the British Rabbit Council. The Argente breeds are generally very gentle, easy going rabbits.[18] The Argente Bleu is bluish-white in color with lavender blue undercolor and blue eyes. Longer dark blue hairs are evenly dispersed in the coat giving a blue tint when viewed at a distance.

The Argente Brun is brownish-white in color with a deep brown undercolor and brown eyes. Longer dark brown hairs are evenly dispersed in the coat giving a brownish tint when viewed at a distance.

The Argente Creme is slightly smaller than the Bleu, Noir or Brun at 2.26kg (5 pounds) adult body weight. The Cremes are also more fine-boned but have the same short, fine rounded ears. Cremes are creamy white with orange undercolor. Longer orange hairs are evenly dispersed in the coat giving a creamy tint when viewed at a distance.

The Argente Noir is fine boned with fine rounded ears and a silky, grayish white body color with deep slate blue undercolor. The coat is sprinkled with longer black hairs that give a muted silver effect when seen from a distance.

Argente Champagne is slightly bigger than the other Argente breeds, with adults weighing 4.53kg (10 pounds). Their ears are slightly rounded and well furred. The body is bluish white and seeded with long jet black hairs that give the rabbit a muted silver appearance at a distance. The ears, muzzle, and nose are slightly darker than the body.

Beige
Beige rabbits are stout but finely boned, similar in personality and body type to the Havana.[4] They have

short, erect ears and dense, silky fur. They are a light sandy or dark chamois color that has a light blue tinge. The hairs are light at the base of the hair shaft and darker at the tips. Their foot pads are blue. Adults weigh 2.26-2.94kg (5-6.5 pounds)

Beveren
The Beveren breed is a strong-boned breed with a long back and a markedly bent profile. The ears are long, erect and well furred. Their eyes match their coat color except white-coated Beverens have blue eyes. Colors seen include blue, white, black, brown and lilac. Adults weigh no less than 3.62kg (8 pounds). Beverens are relaxed and easy going in personality.[18]

Blanc de Bouscat
This breed is quite robust but yet has a long, fine bone structure. They are very energetic and curious rabbits. They weigh 5-7kg (11-15.5 pounds) and the does are slightly larger than the bucks. The fur coat is completely snow white and has a frosty sheen. Eyes are pink like an albino. All breeds of Blanc rabbits are reported to be very curious creatures and gentle in personality.[18]

Blanc de Hotot
Blanc de Hotot rabbits are robust and have a rounded body type. Adults weigh 3.5-4.5 kg (7-11 pounds). They are very energetic and curious rabbits like the other Blanc breeds. Their fur is white, non-pigmented on the body except for the darker colored eye circles. These fine, dark eye circles give the rabbit the appearance of wearing eyeglasses.

Blanc De Termonde
This breed has a long, graceful, muscular body and adults weigh 4.5-5kg (10-11 pounds). The fur is white and of medium length and these rabbits have ruby red eyes.

British Giant
British Giants are large and well-muscled, adults weighing 5.6-6.1kg (12.1-13.1 pounds). They have a broad head and long erect ears. The come in a variety of colors, including white, black, dark steel gray, blue, brown gray and opal. The top of base color is darker than the underfur and many have dark or white bellies. British Giants are affectionate and relaxed, and are not particularly active.[5]

Californian
This rabbit breed was developed in California and they are medium in size, have pink eyes and very dark toenails. They should not have a "mandolin" shaped body. The fur coat is coarse with a dense undercoat. They are white or cream with chocolate, blue, and lilac points. Adults weigh a minimum of 3.4kg (7.5 pounds). Californians are known for being gentle and curious.[6,18]

Chinchilla Giganta
One of the most striking features of the Chinchilla Giganta (Giant Chinchilla) are the black-laced ears. These rabbits are long and graceful with a fine boned head, ears, and legs. Adults weigh around 5.44 kg (12 pounds) and have the typical Chinchilla coloring. The undercoat is deep blue slate colored. Giant Chinchillas are considered to be gentle giants.[18]

Continental Giant
The Continental Giant is an old, impressive, large, solid rabbit breed that stands up in the front. The body length is around 65 cm (26 inches) and adults weigh 5.5-7 kg (12.4-15.8 pounds). They have extremely long, erect ears and the ears should be about 25% of body length. Colors include black, dark steel, light steel, Agouti, Red Agouti, Opal, and Yellow.

Continentals are very intelligent, friendly and are truly

gentle giants.[8] Even though they have gentle temperaments, these very large rabbits can cause injury to handlers when they struggle and kick.[8] The Continental White Giant is similar to the continental giant in size and personality, but the color is white with pink or blue eyes.

Deilenaar

The Deilenaar rabbit is a Dutch breed, medium-sized, short and stocky with little visible neck. The legs are short and cobby. Adults weigh 2.5-3.5 kg (5.5-7.75 pounds) and have a warm red-brown top colored fur (red agouti) with tan-lined, black-laced ears. Wavy ticking is found over the entire body. This ticking is very characteristic of the Deilenaar and gives a "mackerel" appearance. Deilenaar rabbits are lively, affectionate and friendly.[9] From time to time they can be skittish and require room to roam.[9]

Fox Silver

Fox Silvers are medium in size with furry legs and are seen in blue, black, lilac and chocolate base colors. The silver accent comes from silver-ticked guard hairs on the chest, planks, and feet. Adults weigh 2.4-3.1 kg (5.5-7 pounds) and have relaxed personalities.[18]

Havana

The Havana is a compact, stocky rabbit with a very short neck. They have furry, short, pointed ears that sit close together. They are in the Havana color, a rich dark chocolate with a glossy, purple sheen. Adults weigh about 2.7kg (6 pounds). Havana rabbits have the reputation of being very curious and active, but this can vary based on the individual.[18]

Sallander

The Sallander has a very thick, compact body with a broad muzzle. The ears are furry and of medium length. Adults weigh 2.5-4.25kg (5.8-9.6 pounds). The base fur color is pearl with dark brown guard hairs and these give the coat a striking charcoal sheen. This coat coloring is very similar to Chinchilla. The undercolor is white. Sallander rabbits are not widely known as a pet breed and have excitable, active personalities.[16] Females have the tendency to be moody and territorial.[16]

Miniature Satin
These rabbits have a dense, luxurious, satin-like fur texture with a glossy sheen. They are of medium size, adults weighing 1.8-2.2 kg (4-5 pounds). The color is ivory and the eyes are red. Satins are relaxed and easy-going rabbits.[18]

Siberian
Siberian rabbits are medium sized with long, furry, erect ears. The adults weigh 2.26-3.17 kg (5-7 pounds). Colors seen include black, blue, brown and lilac. The shade of color must be the same all over the rabbit with no white hairs present.

Squirrel
Squirrel rabbits are very soft with fine hair, short ears, and moderate sized body. They have a dark slate blue undercolor with "pearling" that gives a distinct gray shine. The eye circles are light pearl-gray and the ears are laced with blue. Adults weigh 2.4-3 kg (5.5-6.75 pounds).

Rex Breeds
The Standard Rex rabbit has a fine, silky coat and are very graceful. The ears are broad, bold and erect. Adults generally weigh 2.72-3.62 kg (6-8 pounds) and come in a variety of colors and coat textures, as outlined below. Smooth and rough-coated Rex rabbits are seen in the following colors: Self- blue, ermine, havana, lilac, nutria and black, Shaded- Sable, Seal Siamese, Smoke Pearl, Smoke Pearl Marten, Tortoiseshell. Tan and agouti patterns also are seen, including fawn, castor, chinchilla,

lynx and opal. Other patterns are also allowed, such as Opossum, Astrex, Dalmatian, Harlequin, Himalayan, Silver Seal, and Satin Rex. Rex rabbits generally are curious and have good-natured personalities.[18]

Mini Rex

The Mini Rex is like a Standard Rex in every way possible except in size. Typically, these petite rabbits are about half the size of a Standard Rex, with adults weighing 1.7-2 kg (3.6-4.5 pounds).

1. All About the Dutch Rabbit. http://www.verlannahill.com/AboutDutch.htm

2. ARBA Recognized Breeds (n.d.). Retrieved June 3, 2013, from American Rabbit Breeders Association, Inc. website: https://www.arba.net/breeds.htm#rabbits

3. Belgian Hare. (2013, March 5). Retrieved June 6, 2013, from Wikipedia: http://en.wikipedia.org/wiki/Belgian_Hare

4. Breed Standards and Colors. (2011). Retrieved June 3, 2013, from British Rabbit Council website: http://www.thebrc.org/standards.htm http://www.thebrc.org/colour-list.php

5. British Giant Breed Information.(n.d.) Retrieved June 6, 2013, from Pets4Homes website: http://www.pets4homes.co.uk/pets4homes/home.nsf/breedinfo/britishgiant

6. Californian Breed Information. (n.d.) Retrieved June 6, 2013, from Pets4Homes website: http://www.pets4homes.co.uk/pets4homes/home.nsf/breedinfo/californian

7. Checkered Giant. (2013, March 31). Retrieved June 6, 2013, from Wikipedia: http://en.wikipedia.org/wiki/Checkered_Giant

8. Continental Giant Breed Information. (n.d.) Retrieved June 6, 2013, from Pets4Homes website: http://www.pets4homes.co.uk/pets4homes/home.nsf/breedinfo/continentalgiant

9. Deilenaar Rabbit Breed Information. (n.d.) Retrieved June 6, 2013, from Pets4Homes website: http://www.pets4homes.co.uk/pets4homes/home.nsf/breedinfo/deilenaar

10. English Angora Rabbit. (n.d.). Retrieved June 4, 2013, from

CHAPTER 8: SPAY AND NEUTER

http://www.raising-rabbits.com/english-angora-rabbit.html

11.   English Rabbit Breed Information. (n.d.) Retrieved June 6, 2013, from Pets4Homes   website: http://www.pets4homes.co.uk/pets4homes/home.nsf/breedinfo/english

12.   Johnson-Delaney, C. (1996). Exotic Companion Medicine Handbook for Veterinarians. Rabbits, 1-12.

13.   Lionhead Rabbit. (2013, May 23). Retrieved June 5, 2013, from Wikipedia: http://en.wikipedia.org/wiki/Lionhead_rabbit#Temperament

14.   Netherlands Dwarf. (2013, May 28). Retrieved June 5, 2013, from Wikipedia: http://en.wikipedia.org/wiki/Netherland_Dwarf

15.   Pollock, A. (2011, November 11). Difference between Holland and French Lop Rabbits. Retrieved June 6, 2013, from Helium website: http://www.helium.com/items/2192169-difference-between-holland-and-french-lop-rabbits

16.   O'Shea, R. (2010, October 6). Rabbit Breed Profiles: The Sallander. Retrieved   June   4,   2013,   from   Yahoo!   Voices   website: http://voices.yahoo.com/rabbit-breed-profiles-sallander-6911934.html?cat=53

17.   Shapiro, A. (n.d.). Lops are Mellow and Other Dangerous Myths. Retrieved June 4, 2013, from the House Rabbit Society website: http://www.rabbit.org/journal/2-10/mellow-lops.html

18.   Size, Personality & Fur Type. (n.d.). Retrieved June 4, 2013, from http://www.hoppitydoda.20m.com/rich_text_5.html

19.   The Polish Rabbit. (n.d.). Retrieved June 4, 2013, from D&D's Bunny Hutch website: http://www.danddsbunnyhutch.com/polishrabbits.htm

20.   What is the Thrianta Rabbit? (n.d.). Retrieved June 6, 2013, from Wise Geek website: http://www.wisegeek.com/what-is-the-thrianta-rabbit.htm

21.   Yun, E. (2008, July 10). Retrieved June 6, 2013, from Yahoo! Voices website: http://voices.yahoo.com/alaska-rabbits-jet-black-rabbit-1618887.html?cat=53

CHAPTER 3
NUTRITION

Before nutrition of the rabbit can be properly discussed, one must understand the process of digestion. The first section of this chapter will be dedicated to discussing the normal digestive system anatomy and physiology of the rabbit. The second section will outline specifics regarding nutritional recommendations and nutritional needs of domesticated rabbits.

Rabbits have a complicated digestive system and their bodies rely heavily on fibrous foodstuffs for nourishment. Rabbits are herbivores and simple-stomached "hind-gut" fermenters.[4,6] The digestive tract's form and function are most like that of the horse.[8] The majority of their digestion occurs in the sections of this "hind-gut" called the cecum and colon.

Rabbits have a symbiotic relationship with gastrointestinal microflora (primarily Bacteroides spp. as well as many other gram-negative bacteria and protozoa) which allows them to break down and ferment tough cellulose in foraged plant materials into an energy source.[8] The microflora also synthesizes important vitamins and proteins for the rabbit.[6] Rabbits select mostly high-fiber foods and few concentrates in the wild. Their specialized digestive tract is able to overcome poor quality proteins found in foraged foodstuffs due to their symbiotic bacterial relationship.[6]

Rabbits spend a large part of the day "grazing" (12-16 hours per day) and they feed primarily at dusk and at night.[2,3,6] Rabbits have large, laterally placed eyes that allow them to have a "panoramic view" for grazing, foraging and being alert for danger. They choose food based off of smell and feel on their lips.[6] Rabbits prefer the most tender parts of high-fiber plant material.[6]

FEEDING BEHAVIOR

Rabbits have very specialized teeth that expertly cut and grind food into a fine paste before it enters the stomach. Rabbits crop the grasses and other forages using a cutting movement with their teeth and move their head side to side, and their bodies in a semi-circular to "zig-zag" fashion as they graze.[3] Rabbits chew very rapidly; the number of jaw movements averages around one-twenty per minute.[3,6] Sunshine stimulates rabbits to graze but cold weather does not stop them from feeding. Grazing speed may be increased if the weather is turning bad or if the rabbit is alarmed.[3] Rabbits are constantly alert during eating and often look up from foraging on the ground. Wild rabbits normally will graze over several acres of territory and keep the vegetation around the burrow very short.[3]

Rabbits mostly engage in what is called "selective feeding" which means that rabbits have a sort of "sweet tooth".[3] This does not mean that they prefer to eat concentrated sweet things, instead they pick the youngest, tender, and most succulent parts of the plant that often contain more readily available starches.[2,3]

DENTITION

Digestion in every domesticated mammal begins in the mouth. Prehension (grasping) and mastication (chewing) of food are the first steps of digestion.

Rabbits have what are called hypsodont (elodont) or open-rooted incisors and molar teeth. These teeth are unique in that they are constantly growing.[6,7]

The dental formula of the rabbit is: I2/1 C0/0 P3/2 M3/3 = 28.[6,7] This formula indicates that rabbits have two sets of maxillary and one set of mandibular ("upper and lower") incisors, no canine teeth, maxillary and mandibular premolars and maxillary and mandibular molars for a total of twenty-eight teeth. There is a small set of incisors behind the maxillary pair, commonly called "peg teeth".[4,7] The premolars and molars are commonly called "cheek teeth" and are indistinguishable from each other.[7]

Their large incisors are designed to cut vegetation. The way the incisors are situated in the front of the mouth encourage them to be constantly sharpened and worn when the rabbit is eating an appropriate diet.[6,7] The incisors grow at 2-2.4 mm per day.[7] The mandibular incisors sit between the shorter first and second maxillary incisor teeth when the jaw is at rest. Longitudinal grooves are present on the buccal (towards the cheek) surface of the incisors and the occlusal ("cup") surface is flat and sharp.[7]

The molars and premolars also have longitudinal grooves on the buccal surface and the occlusal surface are flat and irregular. These irregular surfaces allow for the grinding of fibrous foods.[7] The constant grinding helps to keep the teeth at an appropriate length. The natural fast growth of the teeth together with a poor low-fiber diet will lead to uneven wear of the teeth and can quickly lead to dental problems.[6]

GASTROINTESTINAL (GI) SYSTEM

The digestive tract of the rabbit is long and total gastrointestinal transit time (how fast ingesta moves from mouth to anus) is about eight to twenty-four hours.[4]

Ingesta is swallowed and travels down the esophagus to the simple stomach. Rabbits have simple gastric stomachs, much like horses and humans. Healthy rabbits rarely have an empty stomach.[8] Stomach emptying takes about two hours to complete.[4] Rabbits are unable to vomit due to the well-developed cardiac sphincter muscle where the esophagus meets the stomach. The stomach has three basic sections: the carida, body, and pylorus. The stomach is where ingesta begins to break down more in a chemical fashion as the pH of the stomach is very low, about 1.5 and 2.2. Nursing and young kits have a higher stomach pH (5.0 to 6.5) and it is at this age that the cecum and colon are colonized by microbes. The rabbit stomach is unique in that it does not initiate the myoelectrical peristaltic (rhythmic) movements that move ingesta along the GI tract like that of other mammals.[4,8]

The ingesta then moves from the stomach into the small intestines. The small intestines are very similar to other monogastric (single-stomached) mammals like the horse and human. The small intestines are made up of sections called the duodenum, ileum, and jejunum. There is a unique acute angle near the liver where the duodenum leaves the pyloric section of the stomach and this is a common location for obstructions.[8]

A unique feature of the rabbit small intestines is a round, muscular area at the end of the ileum called the cecal tonsil or sacculus rotundus.[8] This area seems to have an immune system function. In this area is also the junction of the ileum into two structures: the cecum and the colon. This is the second most common site for obstruction in the rabbit GI tract.[8]

The cecum of the rabbit is very large and can hold about 40% of the total volume of the digestive tract.[8] It is a blind-ended sac and at its terminus is a lymphoid structure. The cecum is the primary site of anaerobic fermentation of cellulose and foodstuffs.[3,8] It is here that the symbiotic microbes in the rabbit do their work and cecotrophs are produced.

Ingesta then moves from the cecum into the colon (large intestine). The colon has five sections, including sacculations and other structures that help rapidly separate coarse fiber from more digestible food materials for additional microbial fermentation.[8] It is also in a thickened section of the colon where ganglion cell aggregates called fusus coli are located. This structure regulates the contractions that produce the excretion of normal feces or cecotrophs.[4] Water is also removed from the ingesta at this stage and fecal balls are formed and exit the body via the rectum and anus.

COPROPHAGY

Coprophagy is the eating or ingestion of fecal materials. In some species, this can be a sign of a nutritional imbalance or of a bad behavioral habit but in rabbits, it is quite normal and nutritionally necessary. The type of coprophagy that rabbits engage in is specifically called cecotrophy, as they will ingest cecotrophs regularly, not other types of feces.

Cecotrophs are fecal material have a soft paste-like consistency and a strong characteristic odor.[3] They are often covered in mucus and originate in the cecum of the rabbit. The cecum is a pouch-like structure off of the intestines that contain a particular microbial population. Other animals with cecums include horses and dogs.

Cecotrophs look and feel much different from the typical small, dry, fibrous fecal balls. Cecotrophs are also rarely deposited onto the ground. Cecotrophy occurs in the early morning animals and the process involves the rabbit sitting, bending its head down between its legs and rapidly consumes the cecotrophs directly from the anus.[3] Cecotrophy is also sometimes called "pseudo-rumination."[3]

It is extremely important for rabbits to consume cecotrophs, as nitrogen and certain B vitamins are more readily available for use in the body due to this process. Cecotrophs contain about three times the protein (38.5% vs. 13.6% DM; and more Vitamin K, more B-vitamins than normal rabbit feces.[4] Cecotrophs have a bacteria to ingesta ratio of 1:1. Cecotrophy starts very early in life, as cecotrophs have been found in the stomachs of kits still nursing the doe.[3]

NUTRITIONAL NEEDS

The single most important thing in a rabbit's diet is fiber. Fiber feeds not only feeds the microbes that feed the rabbit, but also facilitate appropriate transit times and gastrointestinal motility. The majority of dental and gastrointestinal diseases of the rabbit can be prevented by feeding an appropriate, high-fiber diet. It has also been shown that a non-digestible fiber component, lignocellulose, has a protective effect against enteritis in rabbits.[8]

The vast majority (75-80%) of the rabbit's diet should be from fiber-rich, high-quality grass hay.[1,3,6] High-quality hay such as oat, timothy, orchard or Bermuda grass, should be offered at will to the rabbit 24 hours a day.[1,8] Alfalfa hay should not be fed to an adult rabbit as it is very high calorie, contains too much calcium, and can be detrimental long-term.[2,3,8]

Commercial pelleted feed provides a small amount of fiber and some protein to the rabbit's daily diet. The pelleted feed should only constitute 10-15% of the total daily diet.[1] Fresh fruits and leafy green vegetables and a commercial rabbit food should be fed daily.

There are several rabbit food mixes on the market that combines pelleted feed and seeds or cereals.[6] These mixes are well liked by rabbits but are very low in fiber and high in carbohydrates and simple sugars. The mixes also encourage rabbits to pick out only the concentrates that they like. If this type of diet is relied upon too heavily, this can lead to unbalanced nutrition, obesity, and GI problems over time.[6] It recommended that these mixes only be fed in very small "treat" sized portions.

Feeding Instructions
• Grass hay, such as oat, timothy, orchard or Bermuda grass should be available to the rabbit 24 hours a day.

• Fresh, high fiber vegetables and leafy greens should be fed daily to all rabbits of all ages.[3,4,5,8]
  ➤ Not to exceed 1 cup per 5 pounds of body weight (250g veg per kilo of body weight)
  ➤ Collards, lettuces, dandelion greens, dill, cilantro, parsley, beet greens, cabbage, spinach, bok choy, Brussels sprouts, carrot tops, endive, summer squash, kale, wheat grass.
  ➤ Offer three different types per day, keep it simple but mix it up to prevent boredom and for optimal nutrition.

• Commercial Rabbit Food – Pellets[3,4,8]
  ➤ Should contain 18-24% fiber, 14-16% protein, and 2% fat.
  ➤ 1/8-1/4 cup per 5 pounds (2.2 kg) body weight

• Fruits and Treats[3,8]
  ➤ 1 tablespoon per rabbit per day
  ➤ Most fruits, including root vegetables: carrot, sweet potato, sweet peppers, blueberries, strawberries, raspberries, apple, peach, plum, pear, melon.
  ➤ Stick will all-natural, whole fruits as the commercial "bunny treats" can be laden with sugar and fat.

Feeding Bowls and Dishes

Rabbits should be fed from heavy ceramic or metal bowls, as these are less likely to be chewed or easily knocked over.[1]

Water Requirements

The amount of water a rabbit needs per day depends on their diet. Most domestic rabbits will consume 50-100 ml/kg/day.[6] Water is best provided fresh daily from a sipper bottle. Bowls can be used as well but are often knocked over or easily contaminated with food, feces or bedding.

WHAT NOT TO FEED RABBITS

It is best to avoid simple carbohydrates, sugar, high fat and high protein foods. These can cause GI upset and excessive gas. Examples include breakfast cereals, grains, nuts, seeds, corn, beans, peas, candy, cookies, breads, grapes, banana, and chocolate.[1,3,8] Cut fresh grass from lawn mowers should never be fed to rabbits as it too can cause a high rate of fermentation and gas, and possibly pesticides and petroleum products.[1] As previously mentioned, alfalfa should not be fed to adult rabbits due to its high calcium and calorie content.[2,8]

1. Brown, D. (2012). Rabbit Handling and Husbandry. WSAVA/FECAVA/BSAVA World Congress. Retrieved June 10, 2013 from Veterinary Information Network (VIN) website: www.vin.com

2. Donnelly, T., Vella, D. (2009, June 29). Abnormal Behavior Problems and Recognition of Pain in Rabbits. Retrieved June 5, 2013 from Veterinary Information Network (VIN) website: www.vin.com

3. Donnelly, T. Vella, D. (2009, April 28). Rabbit Behavior and Husbandry Relevant to Clinical Practice. Retrieved June 5, 2013 from Veterinary Information Network (VIN) website: www.vin.com

4.   Iben, C., Kunzel, F., Handl, S. (2007) Clinical Nutrition in Small Animals (Guinea Pigs and Rabbits), GI Diseases. 17th ECVIM-CA Congress Proceedings. Retrieved June 10, 2013 from Veterinary Information Network (VIN) website: www.vin.com

5.   Johnson-Delaney, C. (1996). Exotic Companion Medicine Handbook for Veterinarians. Rabbits, 1-12.

6.   Kohles, M. (2010) Gastrointestinal Function and Proper Nutrition of the Rabbit. AAVAC-UEP Conference Proceedings. Retrieved June 9, 2013 from Veterinary Information Network (VIN) website: www.vin.com

7.   Lennox, A. (2006). Dentistry of Rabbits. Western Veterinary Conference Proceedings. Retrieved June 10, 2013 from Veterinary Information Network (VIN) website:www.vin.com

8.   Murray, M. (2002) Rabbit Gastroenterology. Western Veterinary Conference Proceedings. Retrieved June 9, 2013 from Veterinary Information Network (VIN) website:www.vin.com

CHAPTER 4
HOUSING

Housing is one of the most important aspects of rabbit husbandry and owner responsibility. In some countries (such as the United Kingdom) laws and Animal Welfare Acts require rabbit owners to meet their pet's needs in a fairly specific manner.[5] Basic welfare needs include providing a suitable environment, appropriate diet, environmental enrichment (such as toys, exercise) allowing the rabbit to express normal behaviors, socialization and the company of other animals or rabbits and health.[5]

HOUSING SIZE

The traditional, very small single-housing hutches became popular after World War II as a way to promote growth performance in rabbits kept for meat. These hutches were used in commercial scale meat production and in the gardens of families.[2] This intensive isolation may have produced good results for meat, but it was awful for the rabbit's well-being. Thankfully, these traditional hutches have fallen out of favor by animal welfare groups, veterinarians, rabbit owners and government entities.[5]

Minimum housing requirements are currently not defined by many animal welfare groups to date, such as the Royal Society for the Prevention of Cruelty to Animals, but others offer basic guidelines. The Indiana House Rabbit Society recommends a minimum size of 30 inches

(76 cm) x 30 inches (76 cm) x 24 inches (61 cm) for a caged 5-6 pounds rabbit, with access to a larger (4 foot x 4 foot or 122cm x 122cm) living enclosure. Most will advocate the bigger, the better and with as many natural elements and/or safe "free-roam" or outdoor access as possible.

Things to keep in mind and accommodate for when selecting appropriate size housing:[1,2,5]

• Height. Rabbits need to be able to sit up completely upright on their hind legs and have clearance between the top of their ears and the roof of the cage.

• Exercise. The enclosure or cage should have enough space to turn around unhindered, stretch out their legs fully in any direction, run, or take several uninterrupted hops in any direction. Rabbits naturally forage and are active in the early morning, at dusk and at night.[2] It is best to have appropriate exercise space available to them during these times.

• Shelter. Rabbits need a secure shelter to protect them from the weather, predators and a place to hide when frightened. This is especially true in households with dogs, cats, and small children. Housing rabbits in an appropriate environmental temperature will keep them more comfortable and reduce the chance of heat stress. Temperatures between 16 and 21°C (60.8-69.8° F) are ideal.[4] Protection from the heat must be provided, as heat stress can develop at ambient temperatures above 28 C (83 F).[2]

• Appropriate toilet areas or "latrines." The cage and other exercise or housing areas must have a private, well-ventilated area where the rabbit can use the restroom, such as a litter box. Toilet areas that are without ventilation or

are not cleaned daily can build up an irritating amou
ammonia and wet bedding can predispose skin infections
on the feet.[2] The litter box substrate must be an organic
litter or feline litter such as straw, hay, shredded paper or
paper pellets. Clay cat litters should be avoided as it can
cause gastrointestinal upset and problems such as cecal
impaction if the rabbit ingests the clay.[1,2] The toilet area
should be completely separate from where the rabbit eats,
drinks and sleeps.[5]

• Bedding Substrate. This is one of the most important
features of rabbit housing. The best substrate would be
similar to the texture of natural earth.[2] Wire or slatted
flooring is never recommended, as it predisposes rabbits to
sore feet and can aggravate other health problems like
arthritis.[2,5] Soft bedding such as straw or hay is ideal. These
types of soft beddings materials also will allow the rabbit
to satisfy their natural digging behavior.[2]

HOUSING SET-UP

The best type of housing encompasses a "main shelter"
and a "living enclosure."[5] The benefits of this arrangement
allow the rabbit to have a shelter, a place to hide, and a
safe area to play, forage and get exercise, and rabbits seem
to prefer this as well.[2,5]

Rabbits have a natural instinct to bolt underground into
the burrow when threatened. Having hiding places
available will allow this natural behavior to occur and
greatly decrease the rabbit's stress.[2] Hiding places can be
made using sturdy cardboard boxes or tunnels with
bedding. Rabbit "mazes" can be purchased online and
used as both enrichment (toy) or hiding place. Each hiding
place can be small, but needs two entrance/exit points and
the rabbit should be able to turn around inside of them.[5]
Outdoor or free-roaming rabbits can benefit from

overturned boxes or pipes as hiding places.[2]

Construction and Design

Rabbit housing should be sturdy, protected from drafts, direct sun and/or strong winds. They also need to be predator and escape-proof, provide shade, chew resistant and well-ventilated.[2,5] Water-proofed or preserved materials need to be non-toxic. Using pressure-treated lumber and painted wood is discouraged. Housing needs to be raised above the ground if outdoors, as this deters predators and decreases dampness.[5] Heavy-duty wire mesh walls are appropriate for outdoor housing and be sure that rabbits cannot dig out under the walls.

As mentioned previously, NO wire or barred floors! Rabbits prefer solid, non-slip footing and wire or slotted floors predispose rabbits to sore feet and more discomfort if arthritis is present in geriatric rabbits.[2,5] Line the bottom of the house or cage with appropriate substrate, as discussed previously.

Pre-fabricated cages and exercise areas can easily be purchased at pet stores or online. Indoor or house rabbits can also be easily housed in a converted large or extra-large dog crate; simply remove the door for access to the living enclosure. Dog playpens are also excellent options for living enclosures, many are 30-36 inches (76-91cm) high and prevent even larger rabbits from jumping out.[3]

Location

Rabbits do best in quiet, calm areas of the home or garden and away from household appliances, radios, and loud noises.[5] Rabbits also benefit from unfiltered sunlight and outdoor exercise areas should be considered. Safe outdoor living space, even if only supervised on sunny, mild days, can provide the rabbit with opportunity to stretch his or her legs in a natural environment and allow for natural foraging of grasses and foliage.[2]

Cleaning

Toilet areas must be cleaned daily to prevent ammonia accumulation and health problems.[2,5] The entire home structure should be cleaned with non-toxic cleaning products at least once a week.[5]

HOUSING WITH OTHER ANIMALS

Rabbits are very social animals and enjoy the company of other rabbits, humans and even cats and dogs. As discussed in the Behavior chapter, groupings of castrated sibling (spayed and neutered) rabbits and/or intact females are preferred. Care must be taken when rabbits are housed with dogs or cats, as they can easily harm rabbits. Most often in these "mixed" households, the rabbit becomes the "dominant" animal in the household that demands respect and kindly enjoys the company of others.

1.   Donnelly, T., Vella, D. (2009, June 29). Abnormal Behavior Problems and Recognition of Pain in Rabbits. Retrieved June 5, 2013 from Veterinary Information Network (VIN) website: www.vin.com

2.   Donnelly, T. Vella, D. (2009, April 28). Rabbit Behavior and Husbandry Relevant to Clinical Practice. Retrieved June 5, 2013 from Veterinary Information Network (VIN) website: www.vin.com

3.   Indiana House Rabbit Society.(n.d.) Housing Rabbits: To Cage or Not to Cage. Retrieved on June 13, 2013 from the Indiana House Rabbit Society website: http://www.indianahrs.org/rabbit-care/housing.aspx

4.   Jekl,   V.   (2012)   Rabbit   Behaviour   and   Welfare. WSAVA/FECAVA/BSAVA World Congress Proceedings. Retrieved June 7, 2013 from Veterinary Information Network (VIN) website: www.vin.com

5.   Royal Society for the Prevention of Cruelty to Animals. (n.d.) Rabbits' Housing Needs: RSPCA Companion Animals Pet Care Factsheet. Retrieved June 13,   2013   from   the   RSPCA   website: http://www.rspca.org.uk/ImageLocator/LocateAsset?asset=document&assetId =1232725725160&mode=prd

CHAPTER 5
BEHAVIOR AND TRAINING

Unfortunately, many rabbits every year are abandoned or must be re-homed due to behavior problems.[11] Therefore it is important for every rabbit owner, new or experienced, to be aware of the social needs, normal, and abnormal behavior of the rabbit. It is also of extreme importance that veterinarians and veterinary staff be well educated on the behavioral and social needs of these familiar lagomorphs, in order to be able to help rabbit owners that are struggling with these issues.

First, it is necessary to understand that both European wild rabbits and their domesticated cousins live in a social hierarchy.[11] Wild rabbits live in communities which are called warrens or burrows.[8] These warrens are located under the ground and the rabbits must dig them out with their forepaws. The entrances are small ("bolt-holes"), are located in areas well-covered in vegetation and lead into a network of underground tunnels up to 8-9 feet in depth.[8] These warrens are used for protection, shelter and breeding. When they are used for breeding, they are lined with bedding materials.

Rabbits, wild and domestic, will dig burrows and spend their days hopping, chasing, running and playing in their home territory. As a part of normal, natural behavior, rabbits are very social and amicable behavior is observed such as grooming one another and lying together.[8] Rabbits are largely silent animals, but can make purring, grunting, snorting or "oinking" noises when content or alarmed.[3,14]

Teeth grinding sounds are also common.[3] The "thumping" the ground (noisily stomping the feet) is also observed as an alarm or warning.[14] In less natural conditions, such as a laboratory, hutch or cage, domestic rabbits are still seen exhibiting these natural behaviors, such as digging into bedding.

Normal social structures in wild rabbit colonies revolve around the established territories of the does and dominance hierarchy of the bucks.[8] It is normal during the spring and summer breeding season for older bucks to drive away the younger males that may compete for mates. The most dominant wild males are often the largest and some of the oldest. Older, wild does are often aggressive and territorial around the younger does.[8]

Both wild and domestic rabbits are very social and it is recommended to keep domestic rabbits in pairs.[11] Caged rabbits need to be housed appropriately and have access to an open area ("territory") for exercise outside of the cage. Housing rabbits in an appropriate environmental temperature will keep them more comfortable and reduce the chance of heat stress. Temperatures between 16 and 21°C (60.8-69.8° F) are ideal.[11]

INTER-RABBIT BONDING AND SOCIALIZATION

Littermates and members of a colony are easily bonded in a natural setting. However, when introducing new rabbits to one another in a non-burrow or colony setting special care must be taken. Bonding takes patience and some time. Human supervision is required in order to prevent injuries, but one must take care to not be injured by the rabbits in the process. Having heavy leather gloves on hand and wearing thick footwear will allow separation of fighting rabbits without injury to the handler.[7]

It is best to introduce rabbits to each other when they

han twelve weeks old.[7] When introducing a new s important to start the processes by introducing the rabbits in a new territory (room) in which neither rabbit has been present. This neutral, unfamiliar territory will encourage the rabbits to seek company in the other rabbit. Keeping the rabbits in separate cages but close enough so that their presence is known to each other is important. If the cages are too close, injuries can occur through the wire. Allow each rabbit time alone to explore the new space and after the first is back in its cage, allow the second to explore the same area. This will allow each rabbit to become familiar with the other's scent in the new territory.[7]

Allow the rabbits to approach each other, but be prepared to quickly separate them if a fight breaks out. After several introductions (with no incidents) in the neutral space, they can be left alone together in the new territory. Fighting may occur later, but is much less likely as they begin to bond with each other.[7]

Harnessing each rabbit and introducing them in the neutral territory is also a good method. This allows the rabbit to smell and visualize the other without getting too close. The owner is also physically in control of the rabbits and can pull them apart to avoid fighting and injury. It is best to have the rabbits already used to being on the harness and leash before introductions begin, as this will minimize overall stress.[7] Introducing new rabbits in a bathtub can also be a good method if space is limited inside the home. Place them together in a clean, dry bathtub and give vegetables or hay as a distraction. Bathtubs are slippery and will make it difficult for the rabbits to lunge at each other and fight. Another documented method, although strange, is to put the rabbits in a laundry basket on the floor of a car and drive around in an empty parking lot in tight circles.[7]

Introducing more than two rabbits to each other at a time will increase fighting. Ideal combinations of sterilized rabbit pairs are male/male or male/female and siblings seem to get along better than ones from different litters.[7] Spayed female pairs are more likely to fight. Owners need to be aware that despite introducing their rabbits in a slow, patient and appropriate manner that some individuals simply will never get along. Some rabbits will need to be individually housed as a consequence.[7]

AGGRESSION

Rabbits are not naturally aggressive animals. However, they are able to show aggression in response to fear, territorial, dominance or sexual reasons.[7,11] Aggression is also commonly seen by females feeding kits (lactating) against other kits.[7,11] It is important to realize that the aggression displayed by rabbits in veterinary facilities is most often associated with discomfort, fear, and pain.[11]

It can be difficult for owners and veterinarians to tell the difference between rabbits playing and rabbits fighting out of aggression.[7] Playing often involves sprinting and jumping among young individuals.

Rabbits attack each other (fighting) by running towards the opponent quickly in pursuit. Hopping is often seen in a stiff-legged gait as they move in a half-circle around their opponent. If a retreat does not occur, then the attack may continue. The aggressor then will hold up their haunches and tail, tensing the body and pulling back their ears. This is a typical position for lunging and biting. When rabbits are in this type of body stance, they exhibit snorts, grunts, hissing or harsh barking growls.[7] Thumping with the hind feet is used as a warning, but rabbits can also use thumping to signal danger or dislike of a situation. Rabbits will bite and try to hold onto its opponent with the forelimbs while kicking the opponent with the hind limbs during a fight.[7] This biting and kicking can lacerate the skin, cause damage to external genitalia and even cause evisceration if the abdominal wall is ruptured.

RABBIT-TO-RABBIT AGGRESSION

Typical rabbit-to-rabbit aggression is seen due to dominance, territorial, sexual or maternal reasons.[7]

Dominance

The most common cause of rabbit-to-rabbit aggression is dominance-related. Dominance aggression can be seen in any group of rabbits, regardless of gender, age or neuter status.[7,10] When young rabbits are introduced and housed together at a young age tend to form natural social hierarchies. Problems tend to arise when new rabbits are introduced to a mature rabbit that has been raised and living alone. While it is possible to introduce a new rabbit to a solitary adult, the process can be more difficult. It is often more successful to introduce a new, younger rabbit to an established group of older rabbits.[7]

Sexual

Fighting in intact bucks seems to be more normal for sexual dominance reasons instead of territorial reasons. In this context, fighting may be a "normal" scenario.[7] Young males at puberty tend to become aggressive towards one another, and it is virtually impossible to group males together in the same pens.[7,8] They will chase, kick and bite each other and bite wounds on the testicles are often seen.[4,7] If males are housed together, it is important to provide them with enough space for a male to be able to effectively run away from an aggressive pursuer.[7] Sometimes both dominance and sexual aggression issues can be resolved by creation of compatible groups and neutering.[4,7]

Territorial

In both wild and in domesticated settings rabbits tend to occupy particular areas (territories) and intact adults can be hostile toward younger rabbits within these territories. This can be seen with new rabbits introduced into the household, where the older rabbit with established territory becomes aggressive towards the newcomer.[7] Does can become more territorial during pregnancy or pseudopregnancy and can be heightened during the spring-summer breeding season. These does are not being maternal, they acting in order to protect their territorial assets and resources.[7] Adult males also will acquire their own territories but bucks generally are not as territorial and hostile as does. Territorial aggression can be seen even in bonded pairs or groups when housing is too small or limited; as this can increase competition between individuals for food and sleeping areas.[5]

Dominance and territorial aggression are minimized when young does are raised in a group from a young age. Young females that are raised alone when they are young and then introduced to another new individual or group can react violently and aggressively.[7]

Maternal
Does with kits can display maternally defensive behavior around their nest, but typically do not act aggressively.[7] This dynamic, however, can change if the mothers are housed in groups or are introduced into a new group accompanied by kits.

In a recent study on Swiss breeding farms, it was found that normally group-housed does were housed singly starting twelve days prior to parturition (birthing).[1] After giving birth, the does and kits were re-introduced into groups of eight. In the study, does that were re-introduced into a group with unfamiliar does have more instances of fighting and lesions compared to does that were re-introduced to formerly familiar does.[1] It can be concluded that maternal aggression can be minimized in a group setting if the does are re-introduced to familiar faces, leading to less maternal stress and injury.

Does with kits typically will display aggression towards newly introduced kits. In order to successfully foster kits, it is necessary to camouflage their scent with that of the litter's by placing them on the bottom of the litter pile and rubbing them in the nest bedding.[7]

Other causes

Rabbits will sometimes show aggressive behavior towards other rabbits or humans when they are ill, but this is a much less common cause of aggression.[10] Post-operative and recently stressed rabbits in a veterinary treatment setting can display aggression due to anxiety, pain or fear.[5] Dental occlusions or painful oral trauma can be a common cause of aggression in rabbits.[6] It is of importance for veterinary staff and owners to be aware that the stress related to handling rabbits when sick and post-operative can have lasting effects on learned fear responses to humans and that this stress must be minimized. Appropriate attention to pain management also needs to be ensured to prevent depression, lethargy, inappetence and behavioral changes in these special patients.

Treatment of Rabbit-to-Rabbit Aggression

A certain amount of fighting is expected when rabbits are first introduced. It is of importance to always allow an appropriate amount of space for the newly formed group, with plenty of escape routes available.[7] Larger territory for groups is always better than a small and confined area such as a hutch. Always introduce rabbits in a slow and patient bonding process. Having all members of the group spayed or neutered will also decrease inter-rabbit aggression. If the rabbits are for breeding purposes, neutering the least dominant member of the group can help promote order in the group.

Other important steps in reducing territorial aggression

include providing at least one food bowl per rabbit, well-spaced in the housing territory, avoiding concentrated feedstuffs, and scattering foraging items such as grass, hay and vegetables.[7]

RABBIT-TO-HUMAN AGGRESSION

Aggression towards humans is typically a learned response and can be seen in any rabbit, but it is more common in intact animals.[7] It can be further classified into territorial, food, attention-seeking, or fear aggression.

Most rabbits attack humans for territorial reasons and out of a typical "fight or flight" response.[7] Small or too-small rabbit territory, such as a cage or hutch, can be a predisposing factor. Attacking the human may seem like the only option to the rabbit since small enclosures don't offer an option for running away from the perceived danger. Anger and aggression can be shown when the owner tries to place a food bowl into the cage and the rabbit attacks, biting, head-butting and kicking. Rabbits can also shred bedding or other substrates with their teeth and paws as a sign of aggression, or by picking up objects and flinging them.[7] Rabbits may attack humans when they enter their territory, even if it is quite large. However, when threatened in a larger territory, they will likely thump their feet and run away instead of attacking.[7]

Food aggression, a form of territorial aggression is most commonly seen in small enclosures and with concentrated feeds like pellets.

Rabbits are very social creatures and often will seek out human company in the absence of other rabbits. A common attention-seeking behavior is nipping at the owner's ankles and feet when they feel that they are being ignored. This nipping behavior is not a form of aggression, but owners may interpret it as such.[7]

Fear aggression in rabbits is linked to negative

experiences related to humans. This is seen within household, laboratory, and veterinary settings; wherever the rabbit is most likely to feel afraid or "backed into a corner".[7] Rabbits respond to fear by the typical "fight or flight" response and may learn to not tolerate handling or restraint. Scared or nervous rabbits will flatten themselves to the ground before fleeing or fighting back. Fear aggression can be minimized somewhat if the kits are handled at the time of nursing (approximately fifteen minutes before and thirty minutes after), leading to a reduced fear of humans as they age.[7]

Like in rabbit-to-rabbit aggression, pain can cause aggressive behavior towards adults. Reported causes of chronic pain linked to aggression in rabbits include: dental disease, spondylosis, urinary tract disease, and generalized arthritis. Many owners do not realize that their rabbit may be in pain and may not think of it as a potential cause of the aggressive behavior. In a British study, thirty rabbits out of a hundred and two had dental disease and only six owners were aware of the problem.[7]

Rarely, some rabbits can display normal inter-rabbit and sexual behavior on the humans they are bonded with and this is not a form of aggression. They run circles around the owner's legs, nip, dip and will spray their owners with urine.[10] Spaying or neutering these rabbits will decrease the occurrence of these sexual behaviors but some young rabbits may outgrow this behavior.[10]

Treatment of rabbit-to-human aggression should always begin with a thorough history (context) of when the problems began, how often it occurs, if it involves all humans in the household or just one individual and if it is associated with feeding time. A clinical examination by a veterinarian well-versed in rabbit medicine and surgery is also necessary to rule out sources of pain and underlying disease.[7]

As previously mentioned, early socialization when the rabbit is very young and gentle, appropriate handling throughout life can prevent aggression issues.

BEHAVIOR MODIFICATION

Biting

This type of behavior modification will require several training sessions and slow desensitization over several weeks or months.[7] Place the rabbit in a quiet, neutral territory and wear protective clothing and leather gloves. Ignore the rabbit when it lunges or bites, as this will teach the rabbit that you are not afraid of the biting and that it has no effect.[7] Once the rabbit is quiet, feed it treats while gently petting it. This will teach the rabbit to associate food and good things with your presence and handling. If the rabbit consistently tries to bite you, stroke the rabbit using a long-handled brush.[7] Keep the sessions short and always end them on a positive note.

Rabbit-to-Other Animal Aggression

The most common forms of aggression shown towards other animals in the household include dominance and fear. Rabbits are social animals and may become bonded to other animals (dogs, cats) in the household. It is always recommended that rabbits be supervised when with dogs and cats in the household. Larger predatory animals such as cats and dogs can respond aggressively when the rabbit attacks, which can potentially be fatal for the rabbit.[7] Treatment for aggression towards other animals is difficult and intervention is usually necessary. Allowing a house rabbit to socialize with a guinea pig instead of a dog or cat can be useful. Rabbits may exhibit mounting behavior and dominate the guinea pigs. Housing rabbits and guinea pigs together in the same cage or hutch is not recommended, as they have different nutritional requirements and can share infectious diseases, such as Bordetella bronchiseptica.[7]

Mounting Behaviors

Mounting is often seen between pairs of rabbits as a form of dominance behavior. It can be seen between male, female, or in mixed pairs, sterilized or sexually intact.[9] Separation of the two rabbits is necessary to prevent the behavior from escalating into aggressive and dangerous attacks. Behavior modification for mounting behavior includes spaying or neutering, separation, harness training and slow, patient re-introduction of the rabbits as outlined earlier in this chapter.[16]

STEREOTYPY AND STRESS

Stereotypy is a "pattern of persistent, fixed and repeated behavior that is apparently meaningless" and is often a marker for distress.[7] It is important for owners and veterinarians to be able to identify the signs of stereotypy and respond appropriately to the rabbit. Not all behaviors, normal or abnormal are indicators of distress.

Experts believe that stereotypy can arise from boredom, such as non-stimulating housing, low-sensory input and cage sizes that constrain normal movement. The resulting repetitive behaviors may be done in order to satisfy the rabbit's need for movement or stimulation. Some hypothesize that repetitive movements may be done out of habit once the original source of stress has been removed or eliminated. Others hypothesize that stereotypy may arise as a coping mechanism to "distract" them from other stressors at hand.[7]

One of the most common repetitive behaviors is pawing at cage wires and wire biting in caged rabbits. This most commonly happens in rabbits housed in too-small wire cages and in laboratory environments.[7]

Stereotypy can be prevented by appropriate housing size and environmental enrichment. Changes in these factors and stressors may or may not eliminate problems once they have become chronic or habitual.[7]

DESTRUCTIVE BEHAVIOR

Self-mutilation

Veterinarians often term over-grooming as "non-pruritic alopecia" which means "non-itchy hair loss." Over-grooming can turn into self-mutilation that involves chewing the skin, causing lacerations, ulcers, and scabs. These lesions are often seen on the forelimbs and forefeet.[14]

Over-grooming the fur (barbering) and self-mutilation may be stress, pain or boredom related. Rabbits housed in cages seem to be more predisposed.[3] Rabbits have a natural need to lick and chew things in their environment and can turn it on themselves if there is not an appropriate outlet available.[14]

Nutritional deficiencies and nesting behavior can also cause over-grooming. The first step in treatment includes a physical examination by a veterinarian. The veterinarian will be able to rule out pruritic ("itchy") causes of over-grooming and self-mutilation such as skin mites (not limited to Cheyletiella parasitovorax, Sarcoptes scabiei var cuniculi) or skin infection. Treatment includes identification of possible underlying medical conditions, environmental enrichment (toys, appropriate items for chewing), larger territory, and ensuring that the rabbit is eating a high-fiber, balanced diet.[13] The majority of cases can be successfully treated once environmental and stress related issues are addressed and rabbits rarely need medical treatment (such as anti-anxiety medication).

Chewing

Rabbits are very curious animals and will engage in chewing activities (including tooth-grinding) under normal circumstances when not eating. Common items damaged in the home by chewing include carpet, electrical cords and furniture.[8] High-fiber diets and plenty of distractions such as toys and foraging materials (such as vegetables and hay) can decrease the amount of "negative" or destructive chewing in the home. Electrical cords can be protected with a chew-proof covering and furniture wrapped in a protective covering like cardboard. The best prevention of chewing damage and ensuring that the rabbit is safe is to supervise the rabbit when free-roaming in the house. To discourage rabbits from chewing on household items, use verbal commands (like "no") and spray the offending rabbit with water.[8]

Digging

Digging is a normal behavior that is observed in wild rabbits and domestic rabbits in more natural settings.[3,8,14,15] This urge can be a problem in settings where rabbits are allowed to roam in the house and unfortunately, this natural rabbit behavior cannot be changed.[15]

Common places owners see "destructive digging" includes carpeting and human bedding such as pillows and comforters.[15] Digging can be non-destructive in hutch or cage settings with ample, appropriate bedding. The treatment is prevention, by always supervising the rabbit when free-roaming in the home and protecting favorite digging sites from damage. Paper towels or newspaper in locations of favorite digging spots in the home can provide a safe outlet for digging behavior without causing structural damage.[15] To discourage rabbits from digging in particular locations in the house, use verbal commands (like "no") and spray the offending rabbit with water.[8]

Scent and Chin Marking

Rabbits are territorial creatures and both males and females have specialized scent glands all over their skin. They also have a special scent that is secreted into the urine as well. Rabbits use their scent glands to mark other animals and inanimate objects. These scent glands are anatomically located in the chin, anal glands, inguinal glands (insides of the legs on the belly) and Harderian glands (located near the eyes).[8]

Chinning is when a rabbit marks a surface with secretions from their chin.[3] This is a normal, natural rabbit behavior and is used to mark territory and maintain inter-rabbit hierarchies.[3]

Commonly rabbits will use chinning to "mark" items and humans that they are claiming as their own personal property. This behavior is benign and should not be considered abnormal, aggressive or pathologic.[10] Scent marking on furniture, human bedding, and pillows can cause stains and wear, so it may be necessary to deter the rabbit. Covering favorite marking spots on furniture with cardboard is a good solution and discouraging them by use of verbal commands (like "no") and spray the offending rabbit with water.[8]

REPRODUCTIVE BEHAVIOR

Gestation (length of pregnancy) in the rabbit is thirty to thirty-two days in length.[7,8] A few days before giving birth, the doe will begin to build her nest. She collects hay, straw and other soft bedding materials and assembles them in the nesting location. In the wild, this is done in the warren, burrow or nesting box.[8] She will hollow out the nest as she builds it. Her hair will begin to loosen and she will pluck it from her body and line the nest with this soft material.[8] Once females give birth they will ingest the fetal placenta and membranes. The does will mark their kits with their chin and inguinal gland secretions. Does are very hostile to kits that do not have this mark or scent on them.

If the newborns are not thriving or abnormal, abandonment or cannibalism can be seen. It has been documented that does that build their nests poorly or too late in gestation have a higher instance of litter scattering and cannibalism.[8] Food intake by the mother during or after gestation appears to have no effect on the quality of the nest or rate of cannibalism.[8]

INAPPROPRIATE ELIMINATION

In nature, wild rabbits are very tidy when dealing with fecal and urine waste products. They use specific locations near the warren or burrow as their toilet or "latrine."[8] Often these are a foot or more in diameter and circular in shape with dry fecal pellets at the center. Domestic rabbits tend to select a latrine site in one particular location, such as in the corner of the hutch or cage. They will also leave randomly distributed fecal pellets in their home territory as well.[8]

Inappropriate elimination in rabbits is seen as indiscriminate defecation, urine spraying, and loss of litter box training.[7] Some forms of inappropriate elimination are actually part of normal rabbit behavior as they seek to spread their "scent" in their home territory.

Urine Spraying

Urine spraying in the presence of other rabbits is typically what is called enurination or epuresis, and can occur in rabbit-human interactions. However, most behavior that humans think of as problematic or "abnormal" is actually quite natural for the rabbit. Rabbits naturally will urinate in specific areas (latrines) not only for the sake of voiding themselves but as scent "calling cards" as territorial messages to other rabbits and animals.

Both male and female rabbits can spray urine to mark their territory, and this most often happens on vertical surfaces. Intact mature males spray strong-smelling urine at least ten times more frequently than females.[4] This behavior needs to be addressed as soon as possible to prevent it from becoming a life-long problem. it is very important to have males neutered right at or sexual maturity is reached to prevent urine spraying.

Defecation

Rabbits produce large, dry, fibrous fecal pellets that are laced with the scent gland secretions of the anal glands.[8] As mentioned previously, rabbits (especially bucks) will spread these feces throughout their territory and also in specific "latrine" locations. Even with litter box training, collection of the fecal pellets by the owner, this problem can continue after the buck is neutered and can be very frustrating.

It is important to distinguish inappropriate defecation from uneaten cecotrophs.[8] Problems with cecotrophy can lead to uneaten cecotrophs being left on the floor or matted in the rabbit's fur. Cecotrophy and Coprophagy will be discussed in the next section.

Coprophagy and Cecotrophy

Coprophagy is the eating or ingestion of fecal materials. In some species, this can be a sign of a nutritional imbalance or of a bad behavioral habit, but in rabbits, it is quite normal and expected. The type of coprophagy that rabbits engage in is specifically called cecotrophy, as they will ingest cecotrophs regularly and not other types of feces.

Cecotrophs are fecal material have a soft paste-like consistency and a strong characteristic odor.[8] They are often covered in mucus and originate in the cecum of the rabbit. The cecum is a pouch-like structure off of the intestines that contain a particular microbial population. Other animals with cecums include horses and dogs.

Cecotrophs look and feel much different from the typical small, dry, fibrous fecal balls. Cecotrophs are also rarely deposited onto the ground. Cecotrophy occurs in the early morning animals and the process involves the rabbit sitting, bending its head down between its legs and rapidly consumes the cecotrophs directly from the anus.8 Cecotrophy is also sometimes called "pseudo-rumination". It is extremely important for rabbits to consume cecotrophs, as nitrogen and certain B vitamins are more readily available for use in the body due to this process. Cecotrophy starts very early in life, as cecotrophs have been found in the stomachs of kits still nursing the doe.[8]

TRAINING

Rabbits are social, smart and affectionate animals. They can easily be trained to do simple tasks such as litter box training.

Toilet Training

It is very easy to toilet train a domestic rabbit, as they prefer to use the same area each time for defecation and urination.[8] The owner must simply use a cat litter tray or box where the rabbit chooses to latrine. It is best to keep the rabbit confined to a very small location until it decides where to habitually use the restroom, and then place the litter box. Rabbits will be encouraged to use this new box if the owner spreads a little-soiled bedding into the box.[8] In households with numerous rabbits, many rabbits prefer to use the same communal litter box/latrine area. This behavior is quite different than in cats.

The litter box substrate must be an organic litter or feline litter such as straw, hay, shredded paper or paper pellets. Clay cat litters should be avoided as it can cause gastrointestinal upset and problems such as cecal impaction if the rabbit ingests the clay.[7,8]

Loss of Litter Box Training

House rabbits often can lose or "forget" their litter box training. Like in cats, rabbits can stop using or become reluctant to use their litter box if they feel that it is not safe. This usually occurs if the litter box is in a non-private, high-traffic area of the house. Changes in physical environment (a move, new furniture, etc.), illness and changes in social structure can all disrupt normal litter box habits and training. When a lack of litter box training occurs, re-assess the potential for stressors in the house, have the rabbit medically evaluated, and reinitiate litter box training.[7]

Clicker Training

Any sort of training is accomplished best by positive reinforcement and is a fast way to build a trusting relationship between the rabbit and owner.[2]

Clickers are a form of positive reinforcement that encourages rabbits to continue certain behaviors. Many owners report that you can clicker train your rabbit to do almost any trick or task that the rabbit is physically able to do.[12] Rabbits will learn to associate the click with a reward and in most cases the reward is food.

The general training method is to say or give a command or have the rabbit perform a physical task (such as touching your hand), give a click and then immediately reward with a small treat. Repeat this process until the rabbit reliably hears or sees the command followed by the click and treat.[12]

For example, to teach a rabbit to sit, one should have the rabbit sit, then say "sit", give a click and immediately reward. Many users and advocates promote the use of clicker training to prevent and treat undesirable behaviors in rabbits.[12] Clicker training can be fun, rewarding and will strengthen the bond between owner and rabbit.

More information about clicker training methods for rabbits can be found at www.clickertraining.com.

1.   Andrist, C. Bigler, L. et al. (2012). Effects of Group Stability on Aggression, Stress, and Injuries in Breeding Rabbits. Appl Anim Behav Sci. December; 142(3-4), 182-188.

2.   Bergman, L. (2012, May 20). Clicker Training and Aggression. Retrieved on June 9, 2013 from VIN Vet-to-Vet Behavior Message Board. www.vin.com

3.   Bradley Bays, T.(2009). Understanding & Managing Behavior Problems in Rabbits. Western Veterinary Conference 2009. Retrieved June 8, 2013 from Veterinary Information Network (VIN) website: www.vin.com

4.   Brown, S. (2011, December 6). To Neuter or Not to Neuter Rabbits…That is the Question. Retrieved June 4, 2013 from Veterinary Partner Small Animal Health Series website: http://www.veterinarypartner.com/Content.plx?P=A&S=0&C=0&A=489

5.   Calnon, D. (2008, October 10). Aggressive Behavior from Rabbit Following Castration. Retrieved June 8, 2013 from Veterinary Information Network (VIN) Vet-to-Vet Behavior Message Board: www.vin.com

6.   Denenberg. (2010, May 1). Causes and Prevention of Inter-Rabbit Aggression. Retrieved June 8, 2013 from Veterinary Information Network (VIN) Vet-to-Vet Behavior Message Board: www.vin.com

7.   Donnelly, T., Vella, D. (2009, June 29). Abnormal Behavior Problems and Recognition of Pain in Rabbits. Retrieved June 5, 2013 from Veterinary Information Network (VIN) website: www.vin.com

8.   Donnelly, T. Vella, D. (2009, April 28). Rabbit Behavior and Husbandry Relevant to Clinical Practice. Retrieved June 5, 2013 from Veterinary Information Network (VIN) website: www.vin.com

9.   Eshar, D. (2012, December 11). Two Young Female Rabbits Showing Mounting Behavior and Aggression: Will Spaying or Behavior Therapy Help? Retrieved June 9, 2013 from Veterinary Information Network (VIN) Small Mammal and Exotics Message Board: www.vin.com

10.   Hoefer, H. (2001). Small Mammal Behavior. Atlantic Coast Veterinary Conference. Retrieved June 7, 2013 from Veterinary Information Network (VIN) website:www.vin.com

11.   Jekl, V. (2012) Rabbit Behaviour and Welfare. WSAVA/FECAVA/BSAVA World Congress Proceedings. Retrieved June 7, 2013 from Veterinary Information Network (VIN) website: www.vin.com

12.   Levin, T., Frick, B., Silva, J. (n.d.) Have you Clicked Your Bunny Today? Clicker Training to Address Behavior Problems. Retrieved June 9, 2013 from House Rabbit Society website: http://www.rabbit.org/journal/4-12/clicker.html

13.   Meredith, A. (2008). Dermatological Conditions of Rodents and Rabbits. World Small Animal Veterinary Association World Congress Proceedings. Retrieved June 7, 2013 from Veterinary Information Network (VIN) website: www.vin.com

14.   Pollock, C. (2007) Rabbit Behaviour. British Small Animal Veterinary Congress. Retrieved June 7, 2013 from Veterinary Information Network (VIN) website: www.vin.com

15.   Rosenthal, K., Johnston, M. (2006, November 15). Digging Behavior in Rabbit. Retrieved June 9, 2013 from Veterinary Information Network (VIN) Vet-to-Vet Small Mammal and Exotics Message Board. www.vin.com

16.   Sinn, L. (2013, April 5). Two Young Female Rabbits Showing Mounting Behavior and Aggression: Will Spaying or Behavior Therapy Help? Retrieved June 9, 2013 from Veterinary Information Network (VIN) Vet-to-Vet Small Mammal and Exotics Message Board. www.vin.com

CHAPTER 6
ENVIRONMENTAL ENRICHMENT

Most pet rabbits are kept in a domestic, indoor and non-natural environment. This often unavoidable environment is the top reason that environmental enrichment must be implemented for our beloved pets, in order to ensure a good quality of life. As discussed in the behavior and nutrition chapters, rabbits in a wild or natural setting are very active, social, and spend most of their day foraging. This chapter is a type of extension of the behavior and housing chapters, as many facets of each will be re-visited and expanded. There are also basic recommendations for toys, exercise and other types of enrichment that owners can use to further bond with their rabbits.

EXERCISE

As discussed in the previous chapter, our furry pets' wild ancestors had a very different lifestyle. The normal territory for an adult wild rabbit encompasses about two acres, in which the rabbit forages for food, gets exposure to the sun, runs and interacts with other rabbits outside the burrow.[3,4] Above all, rabbits need exercise more than any type of environmental enrichment. They should not be caged all the time and it is best for them to be able to stretch out and run as often as possible. Many owners are poorly informed and think that rabbits are a great pet because their cage "doesn't take up too much space in the house." Domestic rabbits may seem "happy" and "secure" in their modern burrow (the cage) and seek it out when frightened, but rabbits do not spend all day in the burrow in nature.[3] Keep in mind in that there is no apartment or house size that is too small for a rabbit, they simply need the opportunity in the home to sprint and stretch their legs. Allowing rabbits to "free-roam" on a daily basis in the home or garden may involve more labor (cleaning up scattered feces, rabbit-proofing, etc.) but is worthwhile in promoting a happy, healthy rabbit.

Outdoor exercise is still preferred to indoor for all domestic rabbits. The simplest reason is that an outdoor space like a garden is closest to the rabbit's natural habitat. Rabbits in safe, outdoor settings have an opportunity for beneficial sun exposure and foraging. Studies have shown that rabbits in outdoor play areas actually exercise more than their indoor counterparts in similar-sized pens. This study, although short-term, showed that the larger the pen floor area available the more locomotive activity (physical movement) the rabbits showed, indoors or outdoors.[6]

Allowing daily exercise keeps the rabbit's muscles, bones and metabolism in tip-top shape.[3,4] Rabbits, like humans, that don't get enough exercise are predisposed to osteoporosis (thinning of the bones). It has been shown that rabbits continuously housed in small cages experience poor bone density over time. These thin bones can break easily when the rabbit is handled or even runs or jumps quickly.

Poor muscle tone due to lack of exercise can have equally serious consequences for the rabbit. The most important muscle weakened by lack of exercise is the heart. Rabbits in poor cardiovascular health are more prone to simply dropping dead if stressed (such as being chased by a child or dog) because their heart muscle can't take the strain.[3] Just like with human cardiovascular conditioning, rabbit "couch potatoes" in poor physical condition need to be exercised in a gentle, slow way in small enclosures and gradually graduated to larger spaces in order to prevent injury or sudden death.

Another serious condition that can contribute to poor muscle tone and osteoporosis is obesity. Currently, roughly one-third of all Americans are overweight or obese. Many of our pet species, including rabbits, are following close behind their human owners. Obesity in any species of pet can lead to many health problems including arthritis, urinary tract infections, and shortened lifespan.[5] Like humans, the majority of obese rabbits become so due to a lifestyle lacking in exercise and an inappropriate high-concentrate, low-fiber diet.[3]

Obesity can cause other health problems in rabbits as well. Obese rabbits are more prone to develop "skin fold dermatitis" or inflammation and infection of the skin where fat deposits have created "folds," especially in the dewlap (neck) or perianal area (rear end).[3] Obesity itself can also directly cause nutritional problems and deficiencies in the rabbit. If a rabbit is too fat to physically reach cecotrophs for ingestion, these important nutrients will be missed. Cecotrophs can also complicate skin-fold diseases, if they get stuck in the fur or fatty folds in the perianal area.[3]

Obese rabbits are also predisposed to sore hocks or pododermatitis. This condition occurs when the skin on the feet becomes inflamed and/or infected.[3,4] Sometimes these infections become so severe that they involve the bones of the foot. Excessive weight bearing down on the feet is a cause, as is poor husbandry (dirty or wet bedding), standing on wire flooring or the fact that the rabbit is too fat to properly groom its own feet. Some breeds, such as the Rex or Mini Rex, are predisposed to pododermatitis since they often have extremely thin hair on their feet and don't get adequate foot protection.[3]

There are some genetic factors that come into play regarding obesity in rabbit, but the majority of cases can be prevented with a high-fiber diet and plenty of exercise.

Behavioral issues can often be prevented in rabbits with regular exercise. Normal rabbit behavior is multi-faceted and often involves social interaction with other rabbits or humans. It is difficult and scientifically incorrect to place human emotion on an animal, but it is easy to imagine that rabbits stuck in a cage all the time become "bored" or "frustrated".[3] Rabbits who lack the opportunity to regularly exercise or engage in play are much more likely to show abnormal behaviors like aggression, habitual chewing of cage parts, obsessive grooming, and lethargy.[3,4] Many of these abnormal behaviors can be corrected by simply letting the rabbit exercise and providing stimulating toys and company.

Fun Ways for Rabbits to Exercise
• Let 'em run! Give your rabbit a few hours a day to scurry around in a large, secure area of the house or garden.

• Keep the door open to the rabbit's "cage" as long as possible. As discussed in the housing chapter, allow for a larger "living space" so that the rabbit can take short sprints or several hops in a row.

• Create a "digging box" for your rabbit. These can be made with deeper cat litter boxes or large Tupperware storage containers. Place several layers of newspaper on the bottom along with several sheets of wadded-up newspaper on top. Many rabbits will be entertained for days or weeks shredding and burrowing in this box. The majority of newspaper inks in the United States are non-toxic and vegetable based, but if you're not sure then double check!

• Geriatric rabbits may have a harder time moving around and getting appropriate amounts of exercise. Physical therapy methods such as gentle muscle massage are a great way to keep rabbit muscles healthy, as well as slow exercise. A great way to get your elder rabbit to exercise is to place him or her a little ways from their home and they will slowly, gradually make their way back over the course of the day. You can also create a "bread-crumb trail" out of veggies and other treats.

• Provide toys for the rabbit to roll around and chew on.

• Train your bunny to do tricks or small "tasks." More can be found on this topic in the Behavior chapter.

TOYS

Many rabbits will keep themselves occupied in a domestic setting if they have plenty of hay available for eating, digging in and space to run.[4,9] If space is more limited or unsafe for "free-roam" running, toys are an excellent way for rabbits to pass the time. It has been shown in laboratory rabbits that the presence of toys in the environment leads to considerable more time spent grooming, which is a sign of health and contentment. The rabbits with toys also spent more time grooming themselves or playing with the toys instead of chewing on the cage parts.[8]

Rabbits really enjoy simple, lightweight objects as toys that they can easily push around. A few examples of toys for rabbits include single cardboard rolls (from an empty toilet paper roll), cardboard rings, rubber balls with a bell inside of them, wooden blocks and balls, balls and baskets made from natural wood materials such as Willow branches, woven alfalfa and grass wreaths, "chews" and even some very hard chew toys for dogs like Nylabones.[2,7,8] Some rabbit experts and veterinarians do not recommend artificial, non-digestible toys substrates such as plastics or rubber as they can potentially cause gastrointestinal obstruction.[1] It is also important to ensure that wooden toys are natural, untreated wood or painted with non-toxic paint.

Play and feeding can be accomplished at the same time. The rabbit's daily ration of concentrated feed (pellets) can be put into an old toilet paper cardboard roll, with a few holes cut into it and the ends sealed. Make sure that the holes are big enough for the pellets to fall out as it is rolled on the floor. Many rabbits enjoy pushing around these rolls, getting nourishment, stimulation and exercise all at the same time.

Exercise and toy play can be combined in many of the different "rabbit mazes" that can be constructed at home from sturdy cardboard or purchased online.[2] The mazes provide a sort of cognitive challenge for the rabbit and can be incorporated into a training exercise with the owner. For example, using a clicker and treat rewards, rabbits can learn the fastest way to the center of the maze and ring a bell when they're there, providing entertainment not only for the rabbit and owner but for guests as well.

Exercise and environmental enrichment are not only best for pet rabbits, it is a lot of fun for the owners and can help build a long healthy life and lasting bonds between our two species.

1.   Bennett, A. (2000, August 10). Bunny Toys. Retrieved on June 14, 2013 from Veterinary Information Network Vet-to-Vet Mammals Small and Exotic Message Board: www.vin.com

2.   BinkyBunny. (n.d.) Rabbit Toys and Mazes. Retrieved June 10, 2013 from Binky Bunny website: http://store.binkybunny.com/toys-c2.aspx

3.   Brown, S. (2012, January 13). Rabbits Need Exercise! Small Mammal Health Series. Veterinary Partner. Retrieved June 14, 2013 from Veterinary Partner website: www.veterinarypartner.com

4.   Donnelly, T. Vella, D. (2009, April 28). Rabbit Behavior and Husbandry Relevant to Clinical Practice. Retrieved June 5, 2013 from Veterinary Information Network (VIN) website: www.vin.com

5.   Laflamme, D. (2009). Obesity Management in Dogs and Cats. Western Veterinary Conference. Nestle Purina PetCare Research. Retrieved June 15, 2013

from Veterinary Information Network (VIN) website: www.vin.com

6.   Menbere, S., Hailemariam, M., Hardiman, J., Cooper, J. (2011). 'In or Out?' Encouraging Activity in Pet Rabbits in Outdoor Runs and Floor Pens. Companion Animal Behaviour Therapy Study Group. Retrieved June 13, 2013 from Veterinary Information Network (VIN) website: www.vin.com

7.   Petco. (n.d.). Rabbit Toys. Retrieved June 10, 2013 from PetCo Pet Stores website: http://www.petco.com/N_87_101/Rabbit-Toys.aspx

8.   Poggiagliolmi, S., Crowell-Davis, S. (2008). Environmental Enrichment of New Zealand Rabbits Living in Laboratory Cages. ACVB-AVSAB Conference. Retrieved June 14, 2013 from Veterinary Information Network (VIN) website: www.vin.com

9.   Pye, G. (2000, August 10). Bunny Toys. Retrieved on June 14, 2013 from Veterinary Information Network Vet-to-Vet Mammals Small and Exotic Message Board: www.vin.com

CHAPTER 7
PREVENTATIVE CARE

Rabbit owners are also keen to provide the best preventative care possible for their little loved ones. Across the globe, owners are seeking out the most up-to-date information and rabbit-savvy veterinarians. It is increasingly becoming the veterinarian's responsibility as well to emphasize and promote preventative care and education for rabbit owners. Many veterinarians today are readily able to invest in the additional education and special equipment that is required to provide excellent care for rabbits.[3]

In this chapter, basic preventative veterinary care will be discussed in detail, enabling owners and veterinary professionals to be better able to understand what can and should be done. Awareness of the "normal and content" rabbit will help us determine when our rabbits are "unwell and unhappy."

EXAMINATION AND CONSULTATION

The lifespan of a domestic pet rabbit varies from around five to ten years.[2,3] Rabbit lifespan is continuing to lengthen as better husbandry and medical care is allowing for prevention and successful treatment of disease.[2] Since our rabbit friends age relatively quickly, regular veterinary checks should begin before sexual maturity and should continue every six months for the life of the rabbit.[3] It is not uncommon for geriatric rabbits to require check-ups more frequently. It is difficult to say exactly at what age a rabbit becomes "geriatric" and many pet rabbit experts think this occurs around four to five years of age, or when age-related body changes or disease processes are seen in an individual.[2]

Most veterinarians offer thirty-minute consultations for clients with one to two rabbits present.[9] Every veterinary consultation should begin in the same manner, whether the pet is sick or well. The most important discussion with the veterinarian involves information about the rabbit's health history, housing, diet, and lifestyle. This information can help the veterinarian assess what may be causing a problem if one is found on physical examination (for example, uneven incisor and molar wear secondary to a diet high in concentrates). Many owners find it helpful to make a list of questions for the veterinarian before the consultation and this can help ensure that all facets of care are covered and concerns are addressed.

The veterinarian will perform a basic physical examination and body systems will be evaluated in a manner such as:[2,9]

• Eyes and ears for discharge, excessive head-shaking or head-tilt

• Mouth, tongue, incisor, and molar teeth for wear, ulcerations, etc.

• Dewlap and neck for skin infection, excessive salivation

• Auscultate (listen with stethoscope) heart and lungs

• Auscultate abdomen for gut sounds (or absence of)

• Palpate (feel with hands) abdomen to check for bloating, obstruction, masses, fetuses

• Visually inspect and palpate claws, hocks and feet, clip nails if necessary

• Palpate joints, assess for pain or decrease in range of motion

• Visually inspect perianal area (rear end)

• Properly identify and/or verify sex of rabbit

• Hair coat and skin, checking for mites, fleas or signs of dermatitis

The veterinarian will discuss any abnormalities that were found and make a plan for treatment. At the end of the visit, many veterinarians will offer educational leaflets or handouts on topics of interest such as nutrition or a particular disease process that the rabbit may have currently.[9]

Owners should not hesitate to ask questions or for more information from the veterinarian. Client education is a very important part of ensuring that our pets get the best care possible. The more educated the owner and veterinarians are, the better care the rabbit will receive.

SAFE HANDLING

Proper, safe handling techniques must be practiced at all times to prevent injury to the rabbit and the handler.[1] It is important that all owners and veterinary professionals be aware of the following techniques and to use them consistently. The majority of pet rabbits are used to being handled and are docile, but may become very fearful in a new setting. They may try to run away, freeze in place or attack.[1]

Having a towel handy can assist with especially rowdy rabbits, but it is recommended trying gentle restraint without a towel first. One of the most common positions for handing a rabbit is to "cradle" the rabbit in one arm while stabilizing the head with the other arm with the fingers stabilizing the front feet. Another position is to "cradle" the rabbit by placing one arm under the rabbit, with the arm between the legs and hand holding the front legs, while the rabbit's head is "tucked" into the other arm (or armpit) and the other arm stabilizing the rabbit across the side. Rabbits should never be lifted by their ears. Do not apply too much pressure to the rabbit's chest or abdomen, as this can cause breathing problems and discomfort.[1]

When handling a rabbit on a table, it is best to place both arms along either side of the rabbit's body, with one hand holding the head and using your body against the rabbit's backside – preventing him or her from backing up.[1] Placing a towel lightly over the rabbit's head once it is on the table can make the rabbit feel like he is hidden.

The most common injuries seen in rabbits due to poor handling are to the limbs and spine.[1] Rabbits can quickly kick out if startled, possibly dislocating or fracturing their back (lumbar vertebrae) or falling and sustaining a fracture. These injuries can cause, pain, additional medical care, life-long paralysis and even death.

VACCINATION

Vaccination protocols vary depending on geographic location, the rabbit's lifestyle and other risk factors. It is best to discuss vaccines your rabbit needs with your veterinarian before or at the time of the wellness visit.

The two most commonly given rabbit vaccines throughout the world are for myxomatosis and viral hemorrhagic disease (VHD/HVD). The myxomatosis vaccine is given after the rabbit is six weeks old and the initial vaccination "booster series" encompasses two vaccines spaced two weeks apart. The vaccine is then given every six months during adulthood.[9] Rabbits in endemic areas (such as Europe and Australia) need to be vaccinated against VHD starting at ten weeks of age. The "booster series" encompasses two vaccines spaced two-four weeks apart. Yearly vaccination for VHD is recommended for adults after the "kit series".[3,9] Veterinarians separate the myxomatosis and VHD vaccines and they should not be given within two weeks of each other. Veterinarians currently in the United States and Canada do not vaccinate for myxomatosis and viral hemorrhagic disease (VHD) as they are extremely rare diseases in North America.[4]

Over time, this may change and it is important for veterinarians to be aware of emerging rabbit diseases and the potential need for vaccination in North America. Sporadic, isolated cases of VHD have been reported in the US for over a decade, and a confirmed case of VHD in Canada in 2011, where the diagnosed house rabbit was likely infected by a flying insect vector, prompts us all to be aware of emerging "foreign" rabbit diseases.[6,10]

It is important to read about viral hemorrhagic disease and myxomatosis disease processes the Common Health Problems and Treatment chapter before vaccination.

As of 2013, a new USDA licensed bacterin vaccine for Pasteurella multocida (BunnyVac) is being promoted for the prevention of "snuffles."[5,7] Vaccine development information appears promising and many rabbit breeders and veterinarians are beginning to use the product.

Rabies vaccinations in the US and Canada are considered "off-label" as a vaccine developed for other mammals (such as cats or ferrets) would need to be used. A recombinant or killed virus vaccine should be used.[8] Many veterinarians advocate vaccinating any mammal that spends time outside and may be in contact with roaming or wild animals. Rabies is not a legally required vaccine for rabbits like it is in dogs or cats, but it is a very serious human health concern, so owners need to discuss their family and rabbit's relative risk before vaccination.[11]

Localized injection site (swelling) reactions to vaccines are not uncommon in rabbits. Common signs include mild swelling, redness and mild hair loss at the vaccination site. Gentle massaging the skin around the injection site immediately after the vaccine is given can help decrease reactions.[3] Many vaccines on the market are safe for pregnant rabbits, but it is best to always ask your veterinarian at the time of the visit.

PREVENTATIVE DIET

Rabbit are vegans, so do not feed them anything other than timothy hay, timothy pellets, vegetables, and fruits. Do not feed: nuts, seeds, corn, dairy, cereal, cookies, and bread.

Timothy hay is the most important part of a rabbit's diet and must be fed in an unlimited supply. Alfalfa hay is fine for young rabbits but is not recommended for adult rabbit since it is high in calcium, which leads to bladder and kidney stones in rabbits.

Vegetables are also an important part of a rabbit's diet. Vegetables to provide your rabbit with every day include watercress, lettuce, parsley, carrots, endive, cilantro, Brussel sprouts, basil, and dill. Vegetables high in calcium such as collards, kale, broccoli, spinach, should be avoided since it leads to health problems such as bladder and kidney stones in rabbits.

Rabbit pellets make up a very small part of the rabbit's diet, only about one to two tablespoons daily. Look for pellets high in fiber (minimum 18%) low in calcium (maximum 1%) and low in protein (maximum 14%). The best brand of rabbit pellets available is MARTIN Little Friends Timothy Adult Rabbit Food OR Oxbow Bunny

Basics Timothy Pellets.

Fruit should be fed as a treat, but not too often. You can give your rabbit blueberries, raspberries, strawberries, and apple.

Rabbits produce cecotropes ("night feces"), which are regularly ingested. Cecotropes provide vitamins B and K, amino acids, and fiber.

SPAY AND NEUTER

Spaying and neutering rabbits is a form of preventative care and is recommended for any non-breeding pet. Even if an owner has two or more rabbits of the same sex, sterilization surgery is a good idea. Spaying and neutering prevent uterine, mammary, testicular cancer and other reproductive diseases 100%. It also decreases the amount of fighting or amorous behavior seen between rabbits.[9]

Males must be neutered after three months of age to prevent territorial aggression such as biting. Males are also more likely to get testicular cancer if not neutered.

Females are spayed after five months of age to prevent uterine disorders and reproductive cancers. Some studies show up to 90% of females not spayed get reproductive cancers, eventually leading to death.

PET INSURANCE

Generally, preventative veterinary care (vaccinations, consultation visits, etc.) is very affordable, but costs can quickly add up if a rabbit becomes ill or if an owner has multiple pets. Problems like gastrointestinal stasis can require long hospital stays and medication costs.[9] It is important for owners to look into pet insurance options when they get a new rabbit. Insurance plans can help to decrease costs for wellness, emergency and hospitalization care. Insurance plans vary depending on location and country, it is best to research options online or ask your veterinarian.

If pet insurance for rabbits is not available where you live, it is recommended to be financially prepared by maintaining an "emergency fund" or "health trust" for your rabbit just in case disaster strikes.

GERIATRIC CARE

As pet rabbits are living longer and longer lives, their owners and veterinarians are sometimes challenged by the health problems that all older mammals face. Problems that need to be identified in older rabbits include arthritis, spondylosis, pododermatitis and renal (kidney) failure.[3] Veterinarians must be able to identify problems, assess the quality of life and provide pain management and palliative care when necessary. Many older rabbits enjoy the extra "quality time" that is provided during some of this care and they will develop even stronger bonds with their owners.[3] Common treatments and modifications for the older rabbit include gentle muscle massage and providing shallow litter boxes for easier access.[2]

EUTHANASIA

Assessing quality of life by owners and veterinarians is extremely important in the geriatric patient. Making the decision to euthanize a beloved pet is never easy and sometimes it can be difficult to discuss when "it's time." Many veterinarians begin to introduce the "end of life" topic well before the expected death of a geriatric rabbit.[3] This way, owners, and veterinarians can be more prepared about making an informed decision before the situation gets even more stressful.

The term euthanasia comes from Greek and means a "gentle and easy death." Euthanasia of any pet should be performed in a respectful, caring manner that minimizes stress on the patient and owner. Two phases of sedation and euthanasia technique are recommended, using first sedation or anesthesia prior to euthanasia.[2]

1. Brown, D. (2012). Rabbit Handling and Husbandry. WSAVA/FECAVA/BSAVA World Congress. Retrieved June 15, 2013 from Veterinary Information Network (VIN) website: www.vin.com

2. Carmel, B. (2010) The Elder Rabbit: Care and Welfare of the Geriatric Pet Rabbit. Australian Veterinary Association Proceedings. Retrieved June 12, 2013 from Veterinary Information Network (VIN) website: www.vin.com

3. Carmel, B. (2009). The Healthy Rabbit. AAVAC-UEP. Retrieved June 14, 2013 from Veterinary Information Network (VIN) website: www.vin.com

4. Gentz, N. (2011). October 11. Use of Rabbit Hemorrhagic Disease and Myxomatosis Vaccines for Rabbits. Retrieved June 13, 2013 from Veterinary Information Network (VIN) Vet-to-Vet Mammals Small and Exotic Message Board.

5. Glass, B. (2013, May). BunnyVac Pasteurella Vaccine. Retrieved June 15, 2013 from Mad Hatter Rabbits website: http://madhatterrabbits.files.wordpress.com/2013/05/bunnyvac-bob-glass-qa.pdf

6. Gould, E. (2012, March). First Case of Rabbit Haemorrhagic Disease in Canada: Contaminated Flying Insect, vs. Long-term Infection Hypothesis. Mol Ecol.; 21(5): 1042-7. Retrieved June 13, 2013 from Veterinary Information Network (VIN) website: www.vin.com

7. Hageman, K. (2013, June 8). Source of New Pasteurella Multocida Vaccine for Rabbits (BunnyVac). Retrieved June 15, 2013 from Veterinary Information Network (VIN) Vet-to-Vet Mammals Small and Exotic Message Board: www.vin.com

8. Heard, D. (2013, March 3). Parasite Prevention and Rabies Vaccination for Rabbits. Retrieved June 15, 2013 from Veterinary Information Network (VIN) Vet-to-Vet Mammals Small and Exotic Message Board: www.vin.com

9. King, C. (2012). Rabbit Clinics. WSAVA/FECAVA/BSAVA World Congress. Retrieved June 14, 2013 from Veterinary Information Network (VIN) website: www.vin.com

10. Weese, S. (2011, May 13). Rabbit Hemorrhagic Disease (RHD) Diagnosed

in Pet Rabbit from Canada. Retrieved June 13, 2013 from Veterinary Information Network (VIN) Vet-to-Vet Mammals Small and Exotic Message Board: www.vin.com

11.   Williams, E. (2013, March 1). Parasite Prevention and Rabies Vaccination for Rabbits. Retrieved June 15, 2013 from Veterinary Information Network (VIN) Vet-to-Vet Mammals Small and Exotic Message Board: www.vin.com

CHAPTER 8
SPAY AND NEUTER

In veterinary literature, the scientific terms for removal of the reproductive organs in a male and female of a species are called castration and ovariohysterectomy, respectively. In North America, these procedures are more commonly known to owners as neuter and spay.[2]

SEXUAL BEHAVIOR

Female rabbits are called does and male rabbits are called bucks. Sexually immature rabbits and babies are known as kits or kittens. Sexing a rabbit is quite straight-forward with the animal on its back. The penis of the male is easily visualized overlying the anus with scrotal sacs cranial to the penis. The vulva of the female is immediately cranial to the anus along the dorsum.[6]

Female rabbits, or does, have a duplex-type uterus. The uterus does not have a uterine body; instead, the uterus is divided into two horns. Each horn has a separate cervix that leads into the common vagina.[4] Male rabbits produce spermatozoa (sperm) in two ovoid, equal sized testicles and is housed in a non-pendulous scrotum. Each testis is made up of closely packed seminiferous tubules and the tubules are not subdivided in rabbits as they are in other mammals such as humans.[5]

Rabbits in natural conditions exhibit breeding seasons that are influenced by the length of daylight and temperature.[5] In the Northern Hemisphere, rabbits conceive in the spring and lower conception rates are seen in the fall.

Female rabbits and other lagomorphs do not have reproductive cycles like most other mammals. Estrus behavior, or "heat" may be seen even though the actual estrous cycle does not occur. Rabbits are induced or spontaneous ovulators, meaning that first, the male must mate with the female before ovulation begins. Ovulation occurs approximately ten hours after copulation. Other induced ovulators include the cat and ferret.[5]

Even though female rabbits must be mated before ovulation will occur, they do have a certain rhythm of sexual receptivity, usually every four to six days.[5] They are typically sexually receptive to the male several hours before the time of ovulation.[5]

Courtship can appear as fast, aggressive chasing between rabbits. However, courtship chasing can be distinguished in that when the pursued rabbit is caught, it is not attacked. Once the female is "caught" in the pursuit, courtship continues when the male raises up his haunches and "flags" his tail to her while walking with a stiff-legged gait. He repeats this action for three or four times in succession, sometimes circling her. Many times tail flagging is combined with epuresis. Epuresis or enurination is when the male rabbit emits a stream of urine at the female during the courtship display.[5] Circling the female is very often involved in this process, but it is most common for the buck to run in front of the doe and twist his hindquarters at her while emitting the urine jet. Epuresis can sometimes be a sign of aggression, and this is often seen when the doe enurinates a buck that is pestering her. Epuresis is also used between bucks, such as when an older, more dominant buck is trying to drive off a younger one.[5]

Females in estrus are hyperactive and will react or "flinch" their back when touched. A characteristic sign of estrus in the rabbit is lordosis – the reverse bending and flattening of the back, thus raising the pelvis in a presentation for the male to mount. Females will have an enlarged, red-purple vulva at the time of receptivity.[5] The most reliable indicator of estrus is the visualization of lordosis, and vaginal smears are not helpful in determining when to breed.[5]

Gestation (pregnancy) length in rabbits is approximately thirty to thirty-three days.[4,5] Large breeds can produce up to eight to ten kits per litter and small breeds four to five kits per litter.[5] Rabbits lactate during gestation and sexual desire decreases significantly while kits are nursing.[5]

In one study, 100% of rabbits will mate on the first day after giving birth, 71% on the fourth day, only 42% on the eighth day, and only 11% on the twelfth day.[5] After the twelfth day, all the does studied refused to mate until the young began to feed themselves fifty to sixty days after birth. High sex drive and desire for mating are therefore lost as long as the mammary glands of the domestic rabbit are actively functioning.[5]

Kits are altricial (immature and hairless), active, and able to cast off any remaining birth membranes, suckle, and survive, even if they are not directly attended to by the mother. However, kits for the first few days of life are unable to properly thermoregulate themselves and require the warmth of the mother or external source to survive and thrive.[5]

Rabbits should be spayed or neutered at sexual maturity, which occurs around four to six months of age in small or medium breeds, and around six to nine months of age in large or giant breeds.[2]

Every rabbit should be examined by a veterinarian prior to surgery. During the examination, the rabbit's sexual maturity will be assessed as well as overall health condition. Sexual maturity can be gauged by several methods, including changes in behavior (increased aggression, urine spraying), mature body condition, visualizing testicles and their size in the scrotal sacs, or presence of a well-developed vulva.[2] Unhealthy rabbits should never undergo an elective surgery such as a spay or neuter.

REASONS TO SPAY OR NEUTER

Pregnancy Prevention

Spaying and neutering are the only ways to prevent unwanted pregnancies unless intact males and females are housed completely separately with no interaction. Many veterinarians and rabbit enthusiasts also consider spaying and neutering an excellent responsible and ethical decision, as there are many neglected and homeless rabbits in the world.[2]

Uterine Cancer

Prevention of cancer is the most compelling medical reason to spay female rabbits and other mammalian pet species.[2,4] The most common type of uterine cancer in rabbits is adenocarcinoma, affecting up to 80% of adult intact female rabbits. It is believed that this type of malignant cancer is related to the rabbit's genetic makeup. Adenocarcinomas often quickly spread to other vital organs such as the liver and lungs, causing multiple organ failure and illness. Many veterinary experts recommend having females spayed before they reach two years of age, while cancer instances are small.[2,4]

Uterine Diseases

Adult intact female rabbits can suffer from other uterine diseases besides cancer. Common uterine diseases include pyometra (infected uterus full of pus), uterine aneurism (bleeding uterine vessels) and endometritis (inflamed uterine lining). These conditions are more common in older female rabbits, typically over two years of age.[2,4]

Testicular Disease
Testicular diseases are uncommon but can occur in all intact males. The most commonly seen testicular diseases are abscesses, hematomas, and cancer.[2,4] Abscesses are most common in males that are housed with other intact makes and result from bite wounds to the testicles.[2,4]

Mammary Gland Disease
Mammary gland cancer is closely linked to uterine cancer in rabbits but is fairly uncommon. The most common type of mammary gland cancer is malignant mammary carcinoma. Other common mammary gland diseases include mastitis, cystic mammary glands, and mammary dysplasia.[2,4] Spaying before two years of age greatly decreases the risk of the rabbit developing mammary cancer or other diseases.

Prevention of Undesirable Behaviour
Pseudopregnancies occur when there is a hormonal imbalance after a sterile mating, and the body acts as if it is pregnant but in reality, no pregnancy is present.[2,4,5] False pregnancies last for about eighteen days in the rabbit.[5] This physiological state is not harmful but can be a cause of stress for both the rabbit and her owners. During false pregnancies, females will become territorial, aggressive and spend a lot of energy on nest building. The female's hair will also become loose and she will pluck it from her body to line the nest. An increase in hair loss will occur at the end of the false pregnancy.[5] Some females will also experience a decreased appetite and gastrointestinal upset.[2,4,8] Female rabbits can also develop painful mastitis during or after a false pregnancy.[4] Transportation or stress can induce false pregnancies.[5]

Male and female rabbits can display aggressive behavior after they become sexually mature. To keep this behavior to a minimum or prevent it from happening, it is recommended to have the rabbit spayed or neutered right at sexual maturity. Aggressive behavior typically begins during the "teenage years" between six and twelve months of age. These young rabbits can become destructive and often do not want to be picked up or touched by their owners and attack their cage mates. Often these young rabbits will be seen biting, striking, chasing and lunging at each other.[2]

Urine Spraying

Both male and female rabbits can spray urine to mark their territory, and this most often happens on vertical surfaces. Intact mature males spray strong-smelling urine at least 10 times more frequently than females.[2] This behavior needs to be addressed as soon as possible to prevent it from becoming a life-long problem. As mentioned previously, it is very important to have males neutered right at or after sexual maturity is reached.

Sexually Transmitted Diseases

Rabbit syphilis is caused by an organism called Treponema cuniculi. This is a venereal (sexually transmitted) disease due to spirochete bacteria. Transmission is by genital or extragenital contact on the skin and mucocutaneous junctions such as the external genitalia, chin, lips, face, and nostrils. Signs of rabbit syphilis include tiny vesicles that turn into isolated ulcerations which then turn into crusty, dry, scaly, red areas. Diagnosis is by clinical signs, dark field microscopy, serology, silver stain tissue or mucosal smears. The treatment of choice is penicillin.[8]

ANESTHESIA

The word anesthesia is Greek in origin and means "without sensation."[1] Modern medicine has allowed painful surgical procedures to be performed safely on humans and animals without pain or sensation. The drugs and techniques that are used are being updated and improved frequently in both human and veterinary medicine. Though anesthesia always carries a certain amount of risk to the patient, these risks are continuously being minimized as time goes on.

Simple, short procedures such as venipuncture (blood draws), physical examination and radiography often require anesthetic or sedative agents in many veterinary patients.[3] Rabbits may be difficult to handle without injury to the rabbit or medical team member, and anesthesia allows diagnostics to be performed with as little stress as possible.

Rabbits must be examined and appropriate diagnostics performed (such as blood work or radiography) prior to the procedure in order to perform anesthesia in as safe a manner as possible. Sick or extremely stressed rabbits undergoing procedures may not be good anesthetic candidates, and often procedures are delayed until the patient is stabilized. As a part of the anesthetic plan, an emergency drugs worksheet should always be calculated and ready for each patient and vital signs (heart rate, respiratory rate, blood pressure, etc.) should be continuously monitored by a team member.[3]

Exotics veterinarians and general practitioners with extensive training in rabbit medicine and surgery are aware of the special challenges rabbits present during anesthesia. One thing that should always be taken into consideration with small, easily stressed "prey" animals like the rabbit is the level of catecholamines (such as adrenaline and other stress hormones) present in the body at the time of exam, as this will change how the rabbit physiologically responds to rabbit-specific drug dosages.[3]

General anesthesia allows the patient to be placed in a deeper plane of "sleep" and allows for longer procedures such as spays to safely and painlessly take place. Injectable anesthesia is most commonly used for very short and less painful procedures.

General anesthesia is typically performed by using a combination of injectable and inhalant (gas) agents. It is commonplace to sedate the animal with a "premedication" such as an analgesic (pain medicine) such as a narcotic (butorphanol, buprenorphine, etc.), which will also provide pain relief throughout and after the procedure.[3] The next stage is "induction" of anesthesia, which deepens the plane of unconsciousness (usually with a combination of agents such as ketamine, diazepam, and/or propofol) and allows sufficient relaxation for intubation (placement of a tube into the windpipe).[3] The desired "depth" of anesthesia is then regulated via inhalational anesthetic gas, such as Sevoflurane or Sevoflurane and oxygen throughout the surgical or diagnostic procedure.

Endotracheal (orotracheal) intubation ensures that the airway is protected and that adequate amounts of oxygen and gasses are reaching the patient's lungs at all times. While endotracheal intubation is extremely safe, it can be challenging in the rabbit, due to its small size and unique anatomy. The structures in the back of the throat can be difficult to visualize in the smaller rabbit patient, and often tools like the laryngoscope are helpful for successful, less traumatic intubation. While many laboratory and exotics practitioners may be skilled using a blind technique, direct visualization is preferred.[7]

A recent, small study (thirty-eight rabbits) has shown that nasotracheal intubation is a less traumatic and easier method of delivery of general anesthetic gasses when compared with orotracheal intubation. With nasotracheal intubation, a very small tube is passed through the nasal passages into the nasopharynx and into the trachea. The smaller tube may cause fewer traumas to tissues.[7,9]

Complications of endotracheal intubation in rabbits are uncommon, but can include upper respiratory infection, inflammation, and increased mucosal secretion.[7] The aforementioned small study of thirty-eight rabbits' nasotracheal intubation showed no resulting respiratory complications post-op.[9] As nasotracheal intubation becomes more widely used, we may find that it is a better alternative to orotracheal intubation.

SURGICAL APPROACH

During a male castration or neuter, the testicles are completely removed. There are two castration methods the veterinarian may use for this procedure, the open technique and the closed technique.[8] Each may involve the use of one or two incisions. If one incision is used, it will be placed in front of (dorsal) to the testicles, or two incisions – one placed over each scrotal sac.[2]

Veterinarians very rarely use the open method, due to lack of subdivisions separating and "bundling" the seminiferous tubules and the open inguinal rings of the rabbit.[2,8] If the tunic is incised, the seminiferous tubules will "spill out like spaghetti".[4,8] Use of the closed technique eliminates the risk of incising the tubules or and minimizes risk of intestinal or omental herniation.[2,4]

In the open technique, after the skin incision is made and the testes are retracted. The tunic is cut and carefully stripped down exposing the spermatic cord and blood vessels. The vessels and cord are double ligated and replaced into the incision site after inspection for bleeding.[2] The tunic and/or inguinal ring is then closed with suture and the procedure is repeated on the second testicle and associated structures.[8] The scrotal skin is most often closed with tissue glue. A benefit of the open technique is that the surgeon can visualize that the blood vessels and spermatic cord have been ligated.[8]

The closed technique of castration differs from the open technique only in that the tunic is not incised or opened. The spermatic cord, blood vessels, and tunic are termed the "pedicle" and this is clamped and ligated before the testicle is removed and surgical site closed.[8] The scrotal skin is most often closed with tissue glue. A disadvantage of this method is the chance of a ligature slipping on the vessels due to decreased visualization of the blood vessels.[8]

Twenty-four to forty-eight hours after castration the scrotal sacs will swell, but should quickly resolve in about seven to ten days.[2] It is important to note that male rabbits can still have live sperm living within the section of spermatic cord that cannot be removed during surgery.[2] Newly castrated males should not be put in contact with intact females for three weeks after neutering. Sex drive will still be present in the newly castrated male rabbit, as testosterone blood levels remain high for a couple of weeks after surgery. Take care and monitor the rabbits closely when you re-introduce a post-operative male (or female), since signs of aggression can erupt.[2]

Ovariohysterectomy (OHE) in rabbits is often performed. An OHE in a rabbit is performed much like a cat or dog OHE and there are very few differences. An incision is made onto the skin and through the muscle layers of the abdomen. The uterus is normally visible and surgeons rarely use a spay hook.[8] The double cervix is visualized. The reproductive tract is ligated just distal to the cervix in the thinner vaginal tissue instead of in the thick cervical tissue. The broad ligament should not be stripped out by hand, as the uterine arteries do not lie adnexal to the uterus or cervix, as in the dog or cat. They actually lie to the side in the broad ligament and are ligated separately.[8] Fat storage in the broad and ovarian ligaments can impede visualization of vessels in the rabbit. There is no need to strum on the ovarian ligament, as it is very delicate and easily broken. The ovaries are usually buried in fat and difficult to visualize. The abdominal wall and skin of the rabbit are closed in the same manner as are dogs and cats. Subcuticular suture patterns with absorbable suture are frequently preferred as well as tissue glue, eliminating the need for suture removal.[2,8]

It is recommended that all female reproductive organs be removed at the time of spay (ovaries, cervixes, and uterine horns) despite the fact that some veterinarians are now advocating the removal of only the ovaries.[2] This is a controversial topic and it is still unknown if uterine cancer can be completely prevented or not by only the removal of the ovaries. Uterine cancer is 100% preventable if all the structures are removed during the spay procedure.[2]

POST-OPERATIVE CARE AND COMPLICATIONS

It is important in the two weeks following a spay or neuter to pay close attention to the rabbit's health and incisions.[2,8] It is recommended to check the incision sites at least twice daily.[2] Common complications include incision site swelling and redness, dehiscence (opening of the incision), conjunctivitis, lethargy, anorexia, upper respiratory tract infections, and soft stools.[2,7] If complications such as those listed above are noted, or the rabbit stops eating, acting uncomfortable, not moving or is not producing stools or urine, it is important to contact the veterinary surgeon as soon as possible.

1.   Anesthesia. (2013, May 22). Retrieved June 6, 2013 from Wikipedia http://en.wikipedia.org/wiki/Anesthesia

2.   Brown, S. (2011, December 6). To Neuter or Not to Neuter Rabbits…That is the Question. Retrieved June 4, 2013 from Veterinary Partner Small Animal Health Series website: http://www.veterinarypartner.com/Content.plx?P=A&S=0&C=0&A=489

3.   Divers, S. (2012). Rabbit and Rodent Anesthesia, American Association of Zoo Veterinarians Conference Proceedings. Retrieved June 6, 2013 from Veterinary Information Network (VIN) website: www.vin.com.

4.   Donnelly, T., Vella, D. (2009, June 9). Rabbit Anatomy and Physiology Relevant to Clinical Practice. Retrieved June 5, 2013 from Veterinary Information Network (VIN) website: www.vin.com

5.   Donnelly, T. Vella, D. (2009, April 28). Rabbit Behavior and Husbandry Relevant to Clinical Practice. Retrieved June 5, 2013 from Veterinary Information Network (VIN) website: www.vin.com

6.   Johnson-Delaney, C. (1996). Exotic Companion Medicine Handbook for Veterinarians. Rabbits, 5-6.

7.   Millis, D., Walshaw, R. (1992). Elective Castrations and Ovariohysterectomies in Pet Rabbits. J Am Anim Hosp Assoc, Nov-Dec; 28(6), 491-498.

8.   Rosenthal, K. (2001). Atlantic Coast Veterinary Conference 2001: Rabbit Reproductive Problems and Surgery. Retrieved June 4, 2013 from Veterinary Information Network (VIN) website: www.vin.com

9.   Stephens Devalle, J. (2009). Successful management of rabbit anesthesia through the use of nasotracheal intubation. J Am Assoc Lab Anim Sci. March 2009;48(2):166-70.

CHAPTER 9
HEALTH PROBLEMS AND TREATMENTS

As discussed in the nutrition and preventative care chapters, the majority of rabbit diseases can be prevented by solid, high-fiber nutrition and other health-promoting practices. However, when things don't go to plan it is important to have a general knowledge base of what problems are commonly seen in rabbits and how to treat them.

Conventional veterinary treatments will be discussed briefly, but keep in mind that not all listed treatments are appropriate or available for every individual patient. Medications should only be dosed and given per veterinary instruction and it is recommended that a certified holistic veterinarian is consulted before giving medicinal herbs or homeopathic remedies to rabbits. For example, many homeopathic treatments should be used alone or one at a time due to their potency, and medications like NSAIDs (non-steroidal anti-inflammatory) will block classic homeopathic remedies.[23,40] However, many conventional, alternative, herbal, and homeopathic treatments can be used in a complimentary manner successfully and these treatment modalities are not mutually exclusive.

GASTROINTESTINAL DISEASES

Ileus: Poor Gastrointestinal Motility

Ileus, or gastrointestinal (GI) hypo-motility occurs quite often in rabbits and more so than gastrointestinal obstruction.[24] It is an extremely painful, potentially life-threatening decrease in GI motility and predisposes bezoar formation.[24,39] Its causes must be addressed for prevention and treatment. As discussed in the Nutrition chapter, fiber is necessary to maintain and promote normal GI motility in rabbits. The majority of GI diseases are caused by a combination of low fiber, high concentrate diets, too little exercise and concurrent disease processes. Common concurrent diseases can include dental disease, urinary tract disease, liver disease, stress, chronic respiratory disease, chronic inflammation, and other causes of poor appetite.[39] Stress may decrease motility through action of adrenaline or cortisol on the fususcoli.[32]

Clinical Signs[24,39,42]

- Sudden anorexia or decrease in appetite, weakness, depression, reluctance to move, weight loss, painful abdomen, "hunched" appearance, lack of defecation or a significant decrease in defecation, tooth grinding, increased respiratory rate, increased or decreased borborygmus (gut sounds), hypothermia.

Physical Exam Findings

- Dehydration and painful, distended and "doughy" abdomen. Palpable gas-filled GI tract.

Diagnostics

- Abdominal radiographs (x-rays): visualize gas, rule out obstruction.

- Ultrasound: visualization of decreased or absence of peristalsis (GI motility)

- Complete blood count (CBC), serum chemistry, blood electrolytes, etc.

Treatment[24,39,42]

- Other concurrent and underlying issues MUST be identified and treated appropriately in order to treat and prevent ileus.

- Correct dehydration, if present.

- Pain control: Buprenorphine, butorphanol, flunixin meglamine, carprofen, meloxicam

- Gentle abdominal massage once pain is controlled

- Mild and early cases can be treated conservatively with oral laxatives (such as laxatone) and lubricants (such as mineral oil).

- Placement of fluids and laxatives into the GI tract via an esophageal tube to rehydrate stomach contents.

- Increase the amount of green vegetables being fed to ensure adequate water intake and offer other nutritional support and vitamins (syringe feeding, tube feeding) if the patient is too weak to eat or will not eat.

- Decrease concentrated feeds significantly

- Control enterotoxemia (cholestyramine)

- Promote peristalsis (metoclopramide, cisapride)

- Appetite stimulation (cyproheptadine)

- Anti-gas medications (dimethicone)

- Surgery is NOT recommended for ileus when there is no obstruction present

Alternative and Complimentary Treatments[1,18,23,31,45]

- Herbal Digestive and Liver Tonics[45]
  - ➢ Dandelion root (Taraxacum spp.) - Simulates bile/enzyme production
  - ➢ Yucca root (Y. schidigera) - Improves function of intestinal membranes
  - ➢ Milk thistle seed (Silybum marianum) - Protects and supports liver function
  - ➢ Burdock root (Arctium lappa) - Antioxidant and liver support
  - ➢ Comfrey, strawberry, blackberry leaves - Antioxidant support, regulates GI function[23]
  - ➢ Echinacea - Boosts immune system[23]

- Homeopathic
  - ➢ Borage (gentle laxative), Nux vomica, Ignatia or mycopodium clavatum (decrease gas, calms GI tract)

- Increase the amount of green vegetables being fed to ensure adequate water intake and fiber.

- Vitamins- especially water-soluble B vitamins that promote good GI function.

- Use of digestive enzymes (such as Vetzymes) may benefit rabbits with bezoars, but must be given with care as long-term use can weaken pancreatic function via negative feedback loops.[33]

- Supplemented enzymes such as proteases, bromelain, trypsin and other mixed preparations also have anti-inflammatory properties.[26]

- Pre-biotics & Pro-biotics
  - Prebiotics are non-digestible food ingredients that benefit the host by selectively stimulating the activity or growth of one or more beneficial bacteria in the colon.[13]
  - Probiotics are "live microorganisms which when administered in adequate amounts confer a health benefit on the host" as defined by the Food and Agriculture Organization of the United Nations and the World Health Organization.[13]
  - Lactobacillus
  - Have anti-inflammatory properties[13]
  - Proviable (probiotic)- can be helpful in re-balancing and promoting the healthy functioning of the GI tract.[48]

Prevention
- Feed a high-fiber diet

- Encourage and allow daily exercise

- Appropriate sized housing

- Decrease or prevent stress

GASTROINTESTINAL OBSTRUCTION

Gastrointestinal obstruction in the rabbit can be caused by not only bezoars, but by inadequate food, tumors, adhesions, abscesses, and rarely, foreign bodies.[24] Similarly to rabbits with obstructive bezoars, a low fiber diet can predispose rabbits to GI obstruction and other GI diseases. The distal duodenum and ileocecal junction are the most common sites of GI obstruction.

Clinical Signs[24,39]

- Clinical signs are similar to ileus and bezoars.

- Sudden anorexia, weakness, depression, reluctance to move, weight loss, painful abdomen, "hunched" appearance, lack of defecation, tooth grinding.

Physical Exam Findings[24,42]

- Dehydration and painful, distended and "doughy" abdomen.

Diagnostics[24,42]

- Abdominal radiograph (x-ray) is useful in determining the location of the obstruction.

- Ultrasound is useful in characterizing the obstruction, for example, a tumor versus a cyst or adhesion can be differentiated.

- Complete blood count (CBC), serum chemistry, blood electrolytes, etc.

Treatment[24,42]

- Treatments for ileus, when appropriate.

- Correct dehydration, treat shock, if present.

- Pain control: Buprenorphine, butorphanol, flunixin meglamine, carprofen, meloxicam

- Laparotomy – surgical exploratory
- ➢ Resection of the duodenum commonly occurs in rabbits with obstructions in the distal duodenum, due to tissue necrosis.

- Post-operative: Increase the amount of green vegetables being fed to ensure adequate water intake and offer other nutritional support and vitamins (syringe feeding, tube feeding) if the patient is too weak to eat or will not eat.

- Prognosis of any obstructive disease in rabbits is guarded to poor.[39]

Alternative and Complimentary Treatments[1,18,31,45]

- A partial obstruction caused by something in the lumen of the stomach or intestine may be treated medically if it is likely that it will "move along", but the majority of obstructive diseases are difficult or impossible to treat in this fashion. Most often surgical intervention to relieve the obstruction is necessary. For example, medical treatment (conventional or alternative) is often tried at first for mild cases of bezoars, but if the patient worsens, surgery may be indicated.

- Herbal
- ➢ Comfrey, strawberry, blackberry leaves - Antioxidant support, regulates GI function[23]

- Homeopathic
- ➢ Borage (gentle laxative), Nux vomica, Ignatia or mycopodium clavatum (decrease gas, calms GI tract)[23]

Prevention

- Feed a high-fiber diet

- Encourage and allow daily exercise

- Appropriate sized housing

- Decrease or prevent stress

BEZOARS

Bezoars are one of the more common problems seen in domestic and house rabbits. A bezoar is simply a hairball that has accumulated in the stomach and/or gastrointestinal (GI) tract. Rabbits normally have hair in their digestive systems, as they swallow it as they groom themselves. Hair in the GI tract is not a problem in and of itself, but it can become a problem if other factors prevent it from moving along. Most veterinarians believe that bezoars are typically caused by chronic low-fiber diets and gastrointestinal-related motility issues (ileus) secondary to a poor diet.[39] It is important to note that myoelectrical initiation of peristalsis does not happen in the stomach but in the intestine in rabbits. Due to this naturally weak peristaltic action in the stomach, hair can accumulate in the stomach and may account for many bezoars in rabbits, especially when there is not enough fiber present in the diet. Partial or complete obstructions with hairballs normally occur at the ileocecal junction or distal duodenum.[24]

Clinical Signs[24,39]

- Sudden anorexia, weakness, depression, reluctance to move, weight loss, painful abdomen, "hunched" appearance, lack of defecation, bruxism.

Physical Exam Findings[24,42]

- Dehydration and painful, distended and "doughy" abdomen. Sometimes bezoars can be identified by abdominal palpation.

Diagnostics[24,42]

- When bezoars cannot be palpated, abdominal radiographs (x-ray) and ultrasound are useful in determining the location of the bezoar.

- Complete blood count (CBC), serum chemistry, blood electrolytes, etc.

Treatment[24,30,42]

- Treatments for ileus, when appropriate.

- Correct dehydration, if present.

- Pain control: Buprenorphine, butorphanol, flunixin meglamine, carprofen, meloxicam

- Gentle abdominal massage once pain is controlled

- Mild and early cases can be treated conservatively with oral laxatives (such as laxatone) and lubricants (such as mineral oil) or pineapple juice.

- Placement of fluids and laxatives into the GI tract via an esophageal tube, if indicated.

- Increase the amount of green vegetables being fed to ensure adequate water intake and offer other nutritional support and vitamins (syringe feeding, tube feeding) if the patient is too weak to eat or will not eat.

- Decrease concentrated feeds significantly

- Surgery; when indicated for severe or complete obstructions.

Alternative and Complimentary Treatments[1,18,31,45]

- Herbal Digestive and Liver Tonics[45]
- ➢ Dandelion root (Taraxacum spp.) - Simulates bile/enzyme production
- ➢ Yucca root (Y. schidigera) - Improves function of intestinal membranes
- ➢ Milk thistle seed (Silybum marianum) - Protects and supports liver function
- ➢ Burdock root (Arctium lappa) - Antioxidant and liver support
- ➢ Comfrey, strawberry, blackberry leaves - Antioxidant support, regulates GI function[23]
- ➢ Echinacea - Boosts immune system[23]

- Homeopathic
- ➢ Borage (gentle laxative), Nux vomica, Ignatia or mycopodium clavatum (decrease gas, calms GI tract)

- An increase in the amount of green vegetables may resolve a mild case of bezoars in rabbits.

- Vitamins, especially water-soluble B vitamins that promote good GI function.

- Use of digestive enzymes (Vetzymes) may benefit rabbits with bezoars, but must be given with care as long-term use can weaken pancreatic function via negative feedback loops.[33]

- Supplemented enzymes such as proteases, bromelain, trypsin and other mixed preparations also have anti-inflammatory properties.[26]

- Probiotics- Lactobacillus, (such as Proviable) can be helpful in re-balancing the GI tract of rabbits.[48]

Prevention
- Feed a high-fiber diet

- Encourage and allow daily exercise

- Appropriate sized housing

- Decrease or prevent stress

ENTERITIS COMPLEX

A group of conditions ranging in severity makes up what is known as the "enteritis complex." These conditions range from soft feces to severe diarrhea, enterotoxemia, coma and even death.[39] Most of the time, enteritis is caused by a disruption of normal intestinal flora and is seen secondary to another factor, often external. Enterotoxemia is the most serious presentation of enteritis. Antibiotics, stress (weaning stress), sudden diet change, bacterial overgrowth or concurrent diseases may also be to blame.[15,39]

Pathogenic bacteria such as gram-negative E. coli and Clostridia can also cause enteritis and enterotoxemia. Numerous species of Clostridia are pathogenic and cause enterotoxemia in the rabbit, including C. difficile, C. perfringens, and C. spiroforme. Clostridium spiroforme is especially pathogenic as it produces an iota toxin and leads to high mortality rates (many deaths) in rabbits.[15] Rabbits with C. spirofome infections present with anorexia, depressed and have a bloody to brown watery diarrhea. Rabbits can become quickly hypothermic (low body temperature) and die from this infection.[15,39,42]

Clostridium piliforme causes Tyzzer's Disease in rabbits, rodents, and other mammals. Poor hygiene, stress, high temperatures and overcrowding are predisposing factors.[15,39,42] Watery, hemorrhagic diarrhea and sudden death is seen, especially in young rabbits. Older rabbits may be affected chronically and develop characteristic white military foci in their liver and heart problems due to myocardial degeneration.[39] Tyzzer's Disease is especially difficult to treat due to the fact that C. piliforme has an intracellular stage of its life cycle and rabbits can be asymptomatic carriers. Prognosis is generally poor.

The overgrowth of and disease caused by E. coli is called colibacillosis. Colibacillosis can be readily identified in kits by a watery, yellow diarrhea. 100% mortality is common in these young rabbits due to E. coli.[15,39,42] Older rabbits are less likely to die as quickly from the disease but it can become a chronic problem.

Coccidia
There are about twelve species of the coccidian Eimeria spp. that infect rabbits. (Murray, Garner) Coccidiosis is primarily a disease of young rabbits. E. intestinalis and E. flavescens are the most pathogenic in rabbits, causing foul-smelling diarrhea and sometimes life-threatening dehydration. If the parasite is not found in the gastrointestinal tract, the rabbit may be an asymptomatic carrier or it is infected with the type that lives in the liver, Eimeria stiedae. Eimeria eggs (oocysts) require twenty-four hours or more at room temperature to sporulate before

they become infective.[13]

Pinworms (oxyurids)

Pinworms are very common in pet rabbits. Passalurus ambiguous is the most commonly seen species of pinworm and they live in the colon and cecum.[15,39] Heavy infections may cause the rabbit to be "unthrifty" and has an effect on reproduction. Treatment is often not warranted in healthy rabbits and can be difficult. Ivermectin is ineffective and use of fenbendazole has mixed results.

Clinical Signs[15,39,42]

- Generally: varying degrees of diarrhea – from soft formed stools (mild enteritis) to mucoid, yellow, bloody, brown or blood tinged watery diarrhea (enterotoxemia).

- The color and consistency of diarrhea can be a clue to its cause.

- Depression, dehydration, anorexia, decreased appetite, coma, hypothermia, sudden death.

- Hepatic coccidiosis: weight loss, diarrhea, ascites (free fluid in the abdomen) and icterus (yellowing of mucous membranes and the eyes)

Physical Exam Findings[15,24,42]

- Dehydration, poor body condition, swollen or gassy intestines felt on abdominal palpation.

- Pulmonary edema and congestion

Diagnostics[15,24,42]

- Complete Blood Count (CBC), serum chemistry,

electrolytes, etc.

- Abdominal radiographs (x-ray): The colon and cecum are most often affected in cases of enteritis. Intussusception and prolapse may occur in cases of colibacillosis.

- Fecal culture – anaerobic

- Coccidia, Pinworms: Fecal float and/or direct smear

- Gram stain, Giemsa, silver stains – helpful in cases of enterotoxemia

- Clostridia are easily identified on Gram stains. C. spiroforme has a unique spiral shape

- Histology – from necropsy (autopsy).

- Histologic changes in the colon, cecum and intestines include: swollen enterocytes, heterophilic infiltration, mucosal erosions, bacterial overgrowth, petechae, or dark red/black discoloration of cecum and colon, congestion of GI vasculature

Treatment[15,24,42]

- Correct dehydration, if present.

- Aggressive fluids and supportive care for enterotoxemia
- Clostridial infections: Metronidazole and/or cholestyramine (enterotoxin binding resin)

- Colibacillosis/Pseudomonas: appropriate

antibiotics such as Enrofloxacin

- Tyzzer's Disease: Tetracycline or Oxytetracycline

- Coccidia: Trimethoprim potentiated sulfa drugs for a ten-day duration and supportive care

- Pinworms: Often not treated due to mixed results with dewormers.

- Appropriate nutritional support with vitamins: Increase the amount of green vegetables being fed to ensure adequate water intake. Syringe feeding, tube feeding if the patient is too weak to eat or will not eat.

Alternative and Complimentary Treatments[1,18,31,45]
- Herbal Digestive and Liver Tonics[45]
- ➢ Dandelion root (Taraxacum spp.) - Simulates bile/enzyme production
- ➢ Yucca root (Y. schidigera) - Improves function of intestinal membranes
- ➢ Milk thistle seed (Silybum marianum) - Protects and supports liver function
- ➢ Burdock root (Arctium lappa) - Antioxidant and liver support
- ➢ Comfrey, strawberry, blackberry leaves - Antioxidant support, regulates GI function[23]
- ➢ Echinacea - Boosts immune system[23]

- Homeopathic
- ➢ Borage (gentle laxative), Nux vomica, Ignatia or mycopodium clavatum (decrease gas)

- Vitamins - especially water-soluble vitamin B12

- Use of digestive enzymes (Vetzymes) as a form of supportive therapy, but must be given with care as long-term use can weaken pancreatic function via negative feedback loops.[33]

- Supplemented enzymes such as proteases, bromelain, trypsin and other mixed preparations also have anti-inflammatory properties.[26]

- Probiotics- Lactobacillus, (such as Proviable) can be helpful in re-balancing the GI tract of rabbits.[48]

➢ A study in neonatal rabbits showed that after feeding Probiotics (Lactobacillus) in formula that there was a 25% decrease in small bowel colonization by E.coli and a significant reduction in bacterial translocation in the gastrointestinal lymph nodes, spleen, and liver.[33]

➢ The probiotic used in the study mentioned above is available commercially over-the-counter as Culturelle in the US market.

Prevention
- Feed a high-fiber diet

- Encourage and allow daily exercise

- Appropriate sized housing

- Decrease or prevent stress

- Coccidia and Tyzzer's disease: good hygiene

Viral Causes of Enteritis

Coronavirus causes high mortality in three to eight-week old rabbits. Rotavirus enteritis infects nursing kits and often is complicated by secondary E. coli infections. Diagnosis of these viruses can be done by ELISA or electron microscopy methods. Treatment is supportive and identification of secondary bacterial or parasitic causes of diarrhea is crucial for successful treatment of neonates and young rabbits.[13]

Viral Hemorrhagic Enteritis – Calicivirus "European Brown Hare Syndrome"

Viral hemorrhagic disease (VHD/RHD) is an often fatal and extremely contagious disease, with mortality rates (death rates) around 70-100%. European Brown Hare Syndrome is a similar virus with a very similar disease process to RHD but is only seen in Brown Hares.[8,25] It is a very important disease for pet and commercial rabbit owners to be aware of, especially in endemic areas. RHD is caused by a calicivirus, which has two subtypes of a single serotype. Recently a variant of the virus has been identified that caused outbreaks in vaccinated rabbits under thirty days of age. The "classical" virus typically affects rabbits between forty to fifty days of age. The virus is very difficult to culture and study in the laboratory, and thus outbreaks of new variations will have to be controlled and monitored very closely. Incubation period is reported to be between one and three days.[25]

RHD can persist in the environment for a very long period of time and transmission occurs between rabbits by direct contact and by fomites.[8,25] Other mechanical vectors can transmit RHD including biting insects, birds, rodents, or automobiles.[25] The virus is shed in feces and urine for up to four weeks after infection.[25] RHD is endemic in China, Cuba, Australia, New Zealand and most of continental Europe. Sporadic outbreaks have occurred in North America in the last decade, with the most recent isolated case being seen in Canada in 2011, where a pet rabbit was most likely infected by a flying insect vector.[17,47]

Clinical Signs[25]

- Fever
  - ➢ Rabbits die very quickly (within days) of mild lethargy and fever

- Dullness, anorexia, diarrhea

- Rabbits are in good physical form

- Upper respiratory, frothy, blood-stained foam, difficulty breathing

- Diarrhea

- Neurological signs such as paddling, convulsions, incoordination, paddling

- Jaundice (yellowing of mucous membranes and eyes)

- Sudden death

Diagnosis

- Necropsy (post mortem) findings:
- ➢ Hemorrhages of the lungs, trachea, thymus, intestine
- ➢ Black, thickened, enlarged spleen
- ➢ Liver necrosis
- ➢ Dark brown kidneys

- PCR, Western Blot, ELISA from organ tissues

Differential Diagnosis

- Heat stroke

- Acute pasteurellosis

- Enterotoxemia

Treatment
- There is no successful treatment known for RHD

- Supportive treatment can be tried, but fast onset and rapid death can make treatment difficult or impossible.

Alternative and Complimentary Treatments
- Due to the fast onset and rapid deaths of rabbits from RHD, treatment is very difficult to impossible, also taking into consideration foreign animal disease regulations.

- However, there is promising research from China using an immune-stimulating herbal mixture which has been shown to enhance immune response and efficacy of the RHD vaccine.[36] Active compounds from Astragalus membranaceus, Epimedium (yin yang huo), Propolis, and Ginseng.

- Herbal Digestive and Liver Tonics[45]
➢ Dandelion root (Taraxacum spp.) - Simulates bile/enzyme production
➢ Yucca root (Y. schidigera) - Improves function of intestinal membranes
➢ Milk thistle seed (Silybum marianum) - Protects and supports liver function
➢ Burdock root (Arctium lappa) - Antioxidant and liver support

Uncommon Types of Enteritis in Rabbits

Salmonellosis and Lawsonia intercellularis are uncommon causes of enteritis in rabbits, but it is worthwhile testing for these in chronic or unresponsive cases. L. intercellulariscauses "wet tail" disease in hamsters.[15] Diagnosis can be made by histology via Warthin-Starry or Steiner silver stains from deceased rabbits. Chloramphenicol is a published treatment for Lawsonia intercellularis infections (Proliferative Enteriris).[39]

RESPIRATORY DISEASES

"Snuffles", Rhinitis and Pasteurella multocida[6,15,28,30]

"Snuffles" or chronic rhinitis, is an extremely common disease in rabbits. It is most commonly caused by the gram-negative bipolarly staining rod bacteria Pasteurella multocida.[28] P. multocida is a part of the normal bacterial flora of the rabbit's skin, ears, and reproductive tract. Rabbits are predisposed to having problems with this bacteria when they are stressed, have lower immune system function or poor nutrition. Some strains of P. multocida are more pathogenic than others.[15] The most pathologic strains include those from the serogroups A, D and F.[28] P. multocida causes a plethora of upper respiratory, ear, and reproductive diseases, including: chronic rhinitis ("Snuffles"), atrophic rhinitis, ear infections (otitis media and otitis interna), abscesses, bronchopneumonia, abortions, genital infections and acute septicemia.[15,28] P. multocida spreads between rabbits mostly by direct contact but aerosol, sexual and fomite transmissions are possible. "Snuffles" is common in adult and geriatric rabbits and is often a chronic disease that relapses often despite treatment.[5,15]

Clinical Signs

- White discharge from skin & large, white abscesses.

- Nasal discharge, often white in color. Difficulty breathing, chronic sneezing, snuffling, naso-lacrimal duct problems, underlying dental disease, diarrhea, cutaneous or subcutaneous swellings- especially of the neck or face, dirty, painful ears, anorexia, weight loss.

- Head tilts – torticollis

Physical Exam Findings
- Dehydration

- Painful, dirty ears

- Skin or subcutaneous swellings, abscesses, dental disease

- Head tilt- vestibular signs including nystagmus

- Thoracic auscultation: inspiratory/expiratory stertor and stridor

Diagnostics
- Radiographs- skull, dental, thorax

- Bacterial culture and sensitivity

- Rhinoscopy

- Complete Blood Count (CBC), serum chemistry, electrolytes, etc.

Treatment

- Treatment of "snuffles" is most successful when a multi-modal approach is used, including conventional, alternative, holistic and nutritional methods.

- Correct dehydration, if present.

- Enrofloxacin or trimethoprim sulfa antibiotics
  - ➤ Antibiotics are not helpful long-term, especially if an underlying abscess or dental problem is not identified and treated.
- Nebulization

- Drain abscesses and treat with 2% iodine setons

- Appropriate nutritional support with vitamins: Increase the amount of green vegetables being fed to ensure adequate water intake. Syringe feeding, tube feeding if patient is too weak to eat or will not eat.

Alternative and Complimentary Treatments[1,18,31,45]

- Hyperbaric Oxygen therapy.

- Pseudomonas doesn't tolerate high levels of oxygen and hyperbaric treatment may helpfully potentiate several types of antibiotics.

- Nebulization

- Acupuncture – especially for head tilts

- Boost Immune System
  - ➤ Good nutrition
  - ➤ Echinacea, Golden Seal, Systemajuv, Viarstem
  - ➤ Decrease Stress – Bach Flower Homeopathic

Remedy

- Vitamin C

- Probiotics- Lactobacillus, (such as Proviable) can be helpful in re-balancing the GI tract and provide anti-inflammatory support in rabbits.[48]

- Homeopathy[23]
  - ➢ Nosode from the rabbit's discharge
  - ➢ Silicea (stimulates drainage)
  - ➢ Apis mellifica- dilustions of honeybee poison. (decreases edema)[46]
  - ➢ Pulsatilla (decreases purulent discharge)

Prevention

- Feed a high-fiber diet

- Encourage and allow daily exercise

- Appropriate sized housing

- Decrease or prevent stress

- Isolate a rabbit with respiratory signs away from other rabbits, this will help prevent the transmission of P. multocida

- Vaccination – BunnyVac. There is a newly USDA-licensed bacterin vaccine for P. multocida labeled for the prevention of "snuffles." Vaccine development information appears promising and many rabbit breeders and veterinarians are beginning to use the product.[16]

Other Causes of Respiratory Disease in Rabbits[28,30]

Many different bacterial organisms and viruses can also cause upper respiratory disease in rabbits. The more common examples include Staphelococcus areus, Bordetella bronchiseptica, Moraxella catarhalis, Klebsiella pneumonia, myxomatosis ("rabbit pox"), allergy and heat stress.

DENTAL DISEASES

Digestion in every domesticated mammal begins in the mouth. Prehension (grasping) and mastication (chewing) of food are the first steps of digestion.

Rabbits have what are called hypsodont (elodont) or open-rooted incisors and molar teeth. These teeth are unique in that they are constantly growing.[32,34]

The dental formula of the rabbit is: I2/1 C0/0 P3/2 M3/3 = 28.[32,34] This formula indicates that rabbits have two sets of maxillary and one set of mandibular ("upper and lower") incisors, no canine teeth, maxillary and mandibular premolars and maxillary and mandibular molars for a total of twenty-eight teeth. There is a small set of incisors behind the maxillary pair, commonly called "peg teeth."[24,34] The premolars and molars are commonly called "cheek teeth" and are indistinguishable from each other.[34] Their large incisors are designed to cut vegetation. The way the incisors are situated in the front of the mouth encourage them to be constantly sharpened and worn when the rabbit is eating an appropriate diet.[32,34] The incisors grow at 2-2.4 mm per day.[34] The mandibular incisors sit between the shorter first and second maxillary incisor teeth when the jaw is at rest. Longitudinal grooves are present on the buccal (towards the cheek) surface of the incisors and the occlusal ("cup") surface is flat and sharp.[34] The molars and premolars also have longitudinal grooves on the buccal surface and the occlusal surface are flat and irregular. These irregular surfaces allow for the grinding of fibrous foods.[34] The constant grinding helps to keep the teeth at an appropriate length.

The natural fast growth of the teeth together with a poor low-fiber diet will lead to uneven wear of the teeth and can quickly lead to dental problems.[32] Appropriate, high amounts of long-stem fiber must be present in the diet in order for rabbits to chew and maintain good dental health.

The most common dental problems include malocclusion, root elongation, infected teeth and dental abscesses.[32] When the teeth get too long it causes the jaws to occlude improperly and significantly decreases mandibular movement when chewing.[32] Like horses, rabbits can develop "tooth spurs" due to malocclusion and uneven wear. They are sharp edges along the lingual (inside) and buccal (outside) surfaces of the tooth. These tooth spurs cause painful lacerations and ulcers along the inside of the cheeks and tongue and these areas may become infected.[32] Dental disease can lead to gastrointestinal disease, weight loss, pain, oral and facial abscesses, and respiratory disease, including "Snuffles."[15]

Clinical Signs
- Slobbering, facial pain, facial swelling, anorexia, decreased appetite, "grumpiness", weight loss, respiratory signs, perineal caking of feces and cecotrophs.

Physical Exam Findings[6,15]
- Poor body condition

- Skin or subcutaneous facial swellings, abscesses

- Visualization of long tooth roots, malocclusion, uneven tooth wear, oral ulcers or lacerations.

Diagnostics[15]

- Radiographs- skull, dental, thorax

- Bacterial culture and sensitivity

- Rhinoscopy

- Complete Blood Count (CBC), serum chemistry, electrolytes, etc.

Treatment[15]

- Pain control: Buprenorphine, butorphanol

- Periodic crown reduction through burring

- Extraction of maloccluded incisors

- Extraction of infected teeth and bone

- Drain abscesses and treat with 2% iodine setons

- Surgical excision of abscess capsule

- Appropriate systemic and topical antibiotics

- Treatment of concurrent respiratory and/or gastrointestinal disease

- Appropriate nutritional support with vitamins: Increase the amount of green vegetables being fed to ensure adequate water intake. Syringe feeding, tube feeding if the patient is too weak to eat or will not eat.

Alternative and Complimentary Treatments[1,18,31,45]

- Yarrow flower as a topical wound or abscess treatment material.

- Arnica (Arnica montana), Shepherd's Purse for bruising, swelling, blood circulation, promotion of healthy clotting and Comfrey for bone healing.[31]

- Boost Immune System
- ➤ Good nutrition
- ➤ Echinacea, Golden Seal, Systemajuv, Viarstem
- ➤ Decrease Stress – Bach Flower Homeopathic Remedy

- Probiotics- Lactobacillus, (such as Proviable) can be helpful in re-balancing the GI tract and provide anti-inflammatory support in rabbits.[48]

- Homeopathy
- ➤ Nosode from discharge
- ➤ Hypericum perforatum (dulls pain, for nerve damage)[23]

Prevention

- Feed a high-fiber diet

- Encourage and allow daily exercise

- Appropriate sized housing

- Decrease or prevent stress

- Frequent monitoring at home of tooth length and wear and every six to twelve months by a veterinarian or veterinary dentist.

SKIN DISEASES

The skin is important as a physical barrier, sensory, storage (fat), immune and temperature-regulating organ. The basic layers of the skin are the epidermis (most exterior), dermis and hypodermis.[37] Rabbit skin is very thin when compared with cat or dog skin. Their haircoat consists of a short undercoat and longer, coarser guard hairs on top. Some breeds have shorter or longer guard hairs present, such as the Rex or Angora. Rabbits naturally molt twice a year and it starts at the head.[37] Normally hairless areas on the rabbit include the nose tip, inguinal folds, and scrotal sacs. Rabbits lack foot pads like dogs and cats have and their feet are completely covered in fur. The pendulous skin seen under the neck is called the "dewlap" and it tends to be larger in females. Rabbits have five to six pairs of nipples/mammary glands along their ventrum (belly). Rabbit skin lacks sweat glands and they do not pant, both predispose rabbits to heat stress.

Dermatitis

Dermatitis simply means "inflammation of the skin" and it can have many causes in the rabbit, including bacterial, fungal, parasitic, and even secondary to dental problems. Bacterial dermatitis is the most common type of skin problem in rabbits. Lesions can occur anywhere there is skin, including the ears, external genitalia and feet. Pyodermas and abscesses commonly affect rabbits, primarily caused by the following organisms: Pasteurella multocida, Treponema cuniculi, Staphylococcus areus, Pseudomonas aeruginosa, Corynebacterium spp. – Bacterial infections may occur secondary to parasitic or fungal skin diseases.

Clinical Signs

- Pustules, nodules, vesicles, patches, crusts, papules

- Inflamed, red, itchy, dry or moist skin

- Weight loss

- Draining tracts from abscesses

Physical Exam Findings
- Unkempt haircoat, poor body condition

- Itchy skin

- Fever

- Pustules, nodules, vesicles, patches, crusts, papules

- Redness, hot, moist skin = pyoderma
  - ➤ Moist dermatitis is common in overweight rabbits and rabbits with concurrent dental disease
  - ➤ Cellulitis on the ventral neck is likely due to S. aureus or Pasteurella

- Skin or subcutaneous facial swellings, abscesses

- Pasteurella skin infections can turn the skin a blue color

Diagnostics
- Skin scrape, Tape Prep

- Wood's Lamp (UV) examination

- Bacterial culture and sensitivity

- Gram stain

- Complete Blood Count (CBC), serum chemistry, electrolytes, etc.

Treatment
- Pain control, if indicated

- Drain abscesses and treat with 2% iodine setons

- Surgical excision of abscess capsule

- Appropriate systemic and topical antibiotics
  - The majority of bacterial skin infections are caused by Pasteurella, but others may be present.
  - Selection of antimicrobials should be done based off of what bacteria are likely or confirmed to be present by culture and sensitivity.
  - Bathing with a diluted 2% chlorhexidine shampoo may be indicated in severe cases, but care must be taken with handling as severe injury to the rabbit or handler may occur.
  - Treatment of concurrent respiratory and/or gastrointestinal disease
  - Appropriate nutritional support with vitamins: Increase the amount of green vegetables being fed to ensure adequate water intake. Syringe feeding, tube feeding if the patient is too weak to eat or will not eat.

Alternative and Complimentary Treatments[1,18,31,45]
- Yarrow flower as a topical wound or abscess treatment material.

- Arnica (Arnica montana) for bruising and sore muscles[31]

- Boost Immune System
➢ Good nutrition
➢ Echinacea, Golden Seal, Systemajuv, Viarstem
➢ Decrease Stress – Bach Flower Homeopathic Remedy

- Vitamin C

- Probiotics- Lactobacillus, (such as Proviable) can be helpful in re-balancing the GI tract and provide anti-inflammatory support in rabbits.

- Homeopathy
➢ Silicea (for drainage and circulation), Pulsatilla (to decrease purulent discharge)[23]

Prevention

- Feed a high-fiber diet

- Encourage and allow daily exercise

- Appropriate sized housing

- Decrease or prevent stress

- Daily brushing or grooming, especially in long-haired breeds and rabbits with arthritis, who may be painful or have difficulty grooming.

PARASITIC SKIN DISEASES

Fleas (Ctenocephalides felis)

Fleas are the most common parasitic cause of skin disease in the rabbit. Fleas have a fairly simple life cycle and grow from eggs to larvae and then to adults. Fleas typically will lay eggs in upholstery, carpet and in the pet's fur. Fleas are most common in rabbits housed outdoors, allowed outdoor access or are in multi-species homes. Fleas and "flea dander" (black, peppery flea feces) are easily seen on rabbit skin and in the hair. Flea combs are also helpful in identifying adults and flea dander. Skin lesions are typically mild and consist of excoriations, redness and in more severe cases, hair loss and secondary infection.[14] Occasionally, rabbits can develop an allergic dermatitis secondary to flea bites. Fleas may be the most common ectoparasite of rabbits but many others need to be considered when rabbits become itchy and develop lesions.

Sarcoptes spp.

Scabies is a very uncommon cause of skin disease in rabbits, but it has been described.[15] Sarcoptes is very contagious and typically rabbits in mixed households (dogs, cats, humans) are more prone to getting scabies. Affected rabbits are typically very itchy, have popular, red, crusting skin lesions on the legs and ears. Other animals in the household (including humans) may be affected as well.

Cheyletiella spp.

Cheyletiella is known as "walking dandruff" or the "fur mite" of rabbits, cats, and humans.[15] Affected rabbits are mildly itchy, have sometimes excessive skin scaling, redness of the skin and occasionally mild hair loss (alopecia) along the dorsum (back).[15] It is highly contagious and other animals (including humans) can be affected by this skin parasite. These mites are fairly large and have four sets of legs and "hooked" mouth parts. All stages of the life cycle are completed on the host. Undiagnosed mites on a rabbit may be a source of infection for other animals (including people) in the household.

Acariasis - Psoroptes cuniculi

Ear Mites and fur mites (Cheyletiella spp.) are two of the most common ectoparasites in rabbits. Psoroptes cuniculi is the non-burrowing rabbit ear mite and it lives in the epidermis skin layer. The inflammation caused by infection causes severe hyperkeratosis and thick crusts that can occlude the ear canal.[15] The build-up of material in the rabbit's ear causes excessive head-shaking and itchiness. Many times the crusty buildup will not need to be cleaned after appropriate treatment.

Myiasis – Cuterebra spp.

Cuterebra are botflies that lay their eggs in the moist skin of some domestic animals, most commonly cats and outdoor rabbits. The eggs are laid in moist skin of the ventral abdomen (belly), neck and chin and the hatched larvae burrow into the dermis and subcutaneous tissues to feed.[15] The most common diagnostic finding is the "breathing hole" and moist draining tract. The larvae must be very carefully manually extracted. Treatment for secondary bacterial skin infections is often needed.[15]

Parasitic Skin Infections General Information:[6,37]

General Clinical Signs

- Hair loss around lesions or widespread

- Inflamed, red, itchy, occasionally crusty skin

- Excoriations (scratches) and scabs present

- Visualization of parasites, such as fleas

- Draining purulent (pus) skin tracts or ulcers –

myiasis

Physical Exam Findings[15,37]

- Unkempt haircoat, poor body condition, alopecia

- Skin lesions: excoriations, redness, dry crusts

- Signs of secondary bacterial dermatitis or myiasis
- ➤ "Air holes" in the skin and draining tracts – myiasis

Diagnostics

- Visualization and identification of parasite
- ➤ Skin scrape
- ➤ Scotch Tape Prep- Cheyletiella spp.
- ➤ Ear swabs and direct microscopy - Psoroptes cuniculi.
- ➤ Physical Exam

- Wood's Lamp (UV) examination

- Bacterial culture and sensitivity

- Gram stain

- Complete Blood Count (CBC), serum chemistry, electrolytes, etc.

Treatment[37]

- Fleas (Ctenocephalides felis) - Selamectin (Revolution®), topical, once monthly

- Sarcopes spp - Selamectin (Revolution®)

- Cheyletiella spp - Selamectin (Revolution®)

topically or ivermectin as directed

- Psoroptes cuniculi - Selamectin (Revolution®) topically as directed or ivermectin

- DO NOT USE CORTICOSTEROIDS for pruritus (itchy skin) in rabbits[43]

- Treatment of concurrent disease

- Appropriate nutritional support with vitamins: Increase the amount of green vegetables being fed to ensure adequate water intake. Syringe feeding, tube feeding if patient is too weak to eat or will not eat.

Alternative and Complimentary Treatments[1,11,18,31,45]

- Garlic does not harm rabbits when ingested and a tremendous amount of research has been done with garlic in laboratory rabbits. The majority of the data to date has been done regarding anti-inflammatory, blood vessel and thrombosis research.

- Tea tree oil should NOT be used in rabbits, as it is very potent and toxic many mammals, including cats. Neurologic symptoms (seizures, paralysis), hypothermia and vomiting are commonly seen in rabbits treated with tea tree oil.

- Boost Immune System
- ➤ Good nutrition
- ➤ Echinacea, Golden Seal, Systemajuv, Viarstem
- ➤ Decrease Stress – Bach Flower Homeopathic Remedy

- Vitamin C

- Probiotics- Lactobacillus, (such as Proviable) can be helpful in re-balancing the GI tract and provide anti-inflammatory support in rabbits.[48]

- Homeopathy
  > Silicea (for drainage)[23]

Prevention
- Vacuum the house frequently. A cheap, over-the-counter dog flea collar placed inside the vacuum bag or bin will kill any adult, larvae or eggs that are sucked up by the vacuum. Replace the flea collar every two weeks.

- Feed a high-fiber diet

- Encourage and allow daily exercise

- Appropriate sized housing

- Decrease or prevent stress

- Preventative products such as Selamectin as directed

FUNGAL SKIN DISEASES

Dermatophytosis – "Ringworm"
Dermatophytosis is the most common fungal disease in rabbits. Several species can infect rabbits and the species may depend on the rabbit's lifestyle. Microsporum canis and Microsporum gypseum are most common in house or

pet rabbits while Trichophyton mentagrophytes is most common in production, outdoor and wild rabbits.[15,38] The most common skin lesions and clinical signs include localized alopecia ("patchy" hair loss), red skin, brittle hair, and hyperkeratotic (crusty) skin.[15] Diagnosis is made by DTM culture of plucked hairs around the skin lesions. A Wood's lamp (blacklight) exam can be helpful in identifying what hairs to collect, as many species of dermatophyte will turn a "candy apple green" color under a Wood's lamp. The toothbrush method that is often used for collecting hairs for culture in cats can also be useful. Treatment includes topicals like clotrimazole, miconazole, and terbenafine.[15] More severe lesions or disseminated disease should be treated with griseofulvin, itraconazole or ketoconazole. Often these medications can be compounded into a flavored, liquid medication for easy dosing.[15] Bathing in ketoconazole shampoo may be helpful, but may be too stressful or risky for the rabbit. It is important to keep in mind that dermatophytosis is transmissible to other animals and humans in the household and environmental "decontamination" (steam cleaning carpets, upholstery, bleaching the rabbit's housing and toys) is necessary.

Pododermatitis – "Sore hocks" or "Bumblefoot"
Wild rabbits live on a variety of surfaces and are able to find softer substrates if needed. With their domestic counterparts, things are not so easy on their little feet. Rabbits don't have foot pads like dogs or cats, their feet are covered instead with a thick layer of hair. This hair, while protective, also doesn't provide enough protection when the rabbit is in an unnatural habitat.[43] Solid flooring and wire floors, while easy to clean and potentially more hygienic, can cause pressure sores on the feet. Often, these sores become painful and infected leading to chronic problems and in severe cases, even death. Pododermatitis literally means "inflammation of the feet" and can occur

on any plantar (bottom) surface of any foot or limb.[5] When the infection is present, bacteria such as Staphylococcus aureus are often to blame.[5] Pododermatitis is most often seen in geriatric rabbits and obese rabbits, and those kept on hard flooring, wet substrate or in unsanitary housing.[5,29] Rex rabbits and mini Rex breeds are predisposed to pododermatitis due to a very thin hair layer on their feet.[38]

Clinical Signs[15,29]

- Alopecia (hair loss)

- Ulcers, red skin, moist, oozing skin

- Scabbed feet and/or hocks

- Cellulitis

- Depression, reluctance to move

- Pain when handled or feet manipulated

- Obesity, Geriatric

- "Grumpy" demeanor

Type Classification/Grading Scale for Pododermatitis in Rabbits[29]

- Type 1
- ➢ Mild, focal lesion of one plantar surface. The fur pad may be thin or missing and the skin is inflamed and thin. No ulceration is present but the skin may be necrotic.

- Type 2
- ➢ More extensive lesion with more severe infection and inflammation than Type 1. These

lesions are typically painful. These lesions bleed easily and purulent (pus) material can be seen.

➢ Late Type 2 lesions can begin to have infection and necrosis spreading into the tendons and other deeper soft tissues of the foot.

- Type 3
➢ Chronic lesions that look like Type 2 lesions, but the tendons, joints and bones are involved. The feet are severely painful and locomotion and function are very limited.

Diagnosis

- Physical exam findings

- Radiographs (x-rays) of feet- sometimes severe cases can infect the tissues and bone of the feet

- Aerobic and anaerobic culture and sensitivity of lesions

- Complete blood count (CBC), serum chemistry, and electrolytes

Treatment

- A grading system has been developed for the evaluation and classification of clinical signs in rabbits with pododermatitis. These grades, or "types" also help the veterinarian decide on appropriate course of treatment.[29]

- Type 1
➢ Aggressive systemic antibiotics
➢ Topical antibiotic or silver sulfadiazine creams

> Pain management
> Prompt correction of husbandry problem
> Keep rabbits on soft, padded, easily cleaned and absorbent surfaces like fleece. Avoid substrates that stick to the lesions.

- Type 2
> Require care mentioned in Type 1
> Surgical debridement of deep lesions and necrotic (dead) tissues.
> Extensive drains, wound management and antibiotic impregnated beads placed into the wounds are often necessary.

- Type 3
> Treatments for Type 1 and Type 2
> Amputation is often indicated at this stage and is necessary to prevent further spread of infection, bacteria in the bloodstream (septicemia), and pain.
> Loss of function is often seen at this stage.
> Euthanasia is often recommended if more than one foot is involved.

- Treatment of concurrent respiratory and/or gastrointestinal disease

- Appropriate nutritional support with vitamins: Increase the amount of green vegetables being fed to ensure adequate water intake. Syringe feeding, tube feeding if the patient is too weak to eat or will not eat.

Alternative and Complimentary Treatments[1,18,31,45]

- Yarrow flower as a topical wound or abscess treatment material.

- Arnica (Arnica montana), Shepherd's Purse and Comfrey for bone healing.[31]

- Boost Immune System
➤ Good nutrition
➤ Echinacea, Golden Seal, Systemajuv, Viarstem
➤ Decrease Stress – Bach Flower Homeopathic Remedy

- Acupuncture (to promote pain relief and circulation)

- Vitamin C

- Probiotics - Lactobacillus, (such as Proviable) can be helpful in re-balancing the GI tract and provide anti-inflammatory support in rabbits.[48]

- Homeopathy
➤ Pulsatilla (decrease purulent discharge)
➤ Silicea (decrease purulent discharge and increase draining)
➤ Magnesia phosphorica (sooths muscle cramps)
➤ Hypericum perfuratum (damaged nerves, dulls pain)[23]

Prevention

- A variety of flooring substrates should be used to allow the rabbit to avoid hard surfaces. A combination of washable, non-toxic fake fur squares, fleece and absorbent pelleted bedding is preferable for all rabbits.[15,29]

- Prevent obesity: feed a high-fiber diet

- Encourage and allow daily exercise

- Appropriate sized housing

- Decrease or prevent stress

- Frequent inspection of the feet of all pet rabbits Especially Rex and Mini Rex breeds

- Daily brushing or grooming, especially in long-haired breeds and rabbits with arthritis, who may be painful or have difficulty grooming themselves.

Myxomatosis[15,38]

Myxomatosis was discovered in research rabbits in South American in the nineteenth century. It has a long history in Australia, where it was used as a biological population control method in the twentieth century. Due to this control method and infection of native populations on other continents, myxomatosis is endemic in Australia, Europe, and North America. This poxvirus is very stable in the environment and is spread by insects and mechanical vectors. Cottontail rabbits (Sylvilagus spp.) are reservoir hosts in North America and European wild, domestic and pygmy rabbits are susceptible to infection and disease.[15]

Clinical Signs
- Skin lesions - raised plaques
  Edematous (skin swellings) on the head, eyelids, and genitals in advanced cases

- Purulent (milky pus) conjunctivitis (inflamed eyes)

- Milky nasal and upper respiratory discharge

- Sudden death

Diagnosis

- Virus isolation, ELISA, PCR, Fluorescent antibody tissue stain

- It is difficult to differentiate Myxomatosis from Shope's fibromas and myxosarcomas by cytology or histology

Differential Diagnosis[15]

- Shope Fibromatosis
- ➤ Caused by a similar poxvirus endemic to the US and Canada but is quite distinct from the myxoma virus.
- ➤ Causes similar lesions
- ➤ PCR should be used to differentiate cases
- ➤ Much milder disease and may spontaneously resolve with supportive care.

Treatment

- Mild cases may recover with supportive treatment

- Many recommend euthanasia to prevent spread to other rabbits, especially since the virus can persist in the environment.

- Severe cases should be euthanized.

- Increase the amount of green vegetables being fed to ensure adequate water intake and offer other nutritional support and vitamins (syringe feeding, tube feeding) if the patient is too weak to eat or will not eat.

Alternative and Complimentary Treatments[1,18]

- Yarrow flower as a topical wound or abscess treatment material.

- Boost Immune System
  - Good nutrition
  - Echinacea homeopathy, Golden Seal, Systemajuv, Viarstem
  - Decrease Stress – Bach Flower Homeopathic Remedy

- Vitamin C

- Probiotics- Lactobacillus, (such as Proviable) can be helpful in re-balancing the GI tract and provide anti-inflammatory support in rabbits.[48]

Prevention

- Vaccination in endemic areas. See chapter on Preventative Care for vaccination protocols and recommendations.
- Insect and vector control in endemic areas.

TRAUMA

Trauma in the pet rabbit most often occurs secondary to the pet being stepped on in the home, shut in a door, mishandled or dropped or attack by another pet. The majority of cases seen are due to improper handling technique (proper handling techniques are discussed in the Preventative Care chapter). Most often rabbits will kick out and twist their backs, leading to lumbar spine dislocation or fracture. Severe back injuries can also lead to urinary incontinence and problems with proper bladder function such as bladder atony. Obese rabbits in poor muscle condition and rabbits with osteoporosis are also prone to bone fracture.[4]

Diagnosis

- Radiographs are necessary after any traumatic event, in order to localize where the problem is (especially fractures of the spine and other bones) and determine the course of treatment and prognosis.

- Some rabbits are able to be treated after a lumbar injury, but many are euthanized if the spinal cord is severely damaged.

Treatment

- Bandaging, wound care, or surgery depending on the extent of injuries and location.

- Medical and supportive care should be given for bone and soft tissue injuries with pain management.

Alternative and Complimentary Treatments

- Control of bruising and bleeding
- Arnica (Arnica montana)
- Shepherd's Purse and Comfrey for bone healing.[31]

- Acupuncture and aquapuncture with vitamin B12 or homeopathics
- Pain relief, stimulating circulation and treating neurologic bladder atony.

- Homeopathy

➢ Zeel and/or traumeel in dilution[20,23]
➢ Hypericum perforatum (damaged nerves, pain killer)
➢ Magnesia phosphorica (soothes muscle cramps)

URINARY DISEASES

Rabbits may be prone to urinary diseases if they are fed an improper diet or an imbalanced diet. Infection and genetics can also play an important role. The most common urinary problem that rabbits present with is urinary bladder "sludge" or calculi. Some rabbits develop calcium carbonate deposits in their urinary bladder and some of these can appear as a fine "sediment or sand" or even larger bladder "stones." Bladder sediment is a common finding in rabbits with gastrointestinal stasis.[43] Many times these deposits and stones are very irritating to the rabbit but bacterial urinary tract or bladder infections are rarely seen in the rabbit. Results of a urine culture and sensitivity should be obtained before starting a rabbit on antibiotics for a UTI.[43] Calcium in the urine of rabbits can be a normal finding as well. If a rabbit's urine looks a little whitish and is not having any clinical signs of urinary problems, this is likely normal urine for this particular rabbit.

Clinical Signs
- Difficulty urinating, straining to urinate

- Urine scald on the skin around penis or vulva

- Anorexia or inappetence

- Lethargy

- Painful abdomen

- Sometimes a solid mass can be felt in the bladder on abdominal palpation[43]

Diagnosis

- Abdominal radiograph
- ➢ Calcium deposits are easily visualized on x-ray

- Ultrasound
- ➢ Abdominal ultrasound can be helpful to determine if and where a stone is located in the urethra

- A rabbit should not go to surgery for a bladder stone simply due to deposits being seen on radiographs. Confirm the presence of actual stones (and not just sand) on ultrasound and/or by palpation.[43]

Treatment

- Subcutaneous fluids- helps dilute the urine

- Pain management

- NO ALFALFA – high in calcium

- Good supportive nutrition

- Treatment of urine scald, if present

- A urine culture and sensitivity should be obtained before starting a rabbit on antibiotics for a UTI.

- Hydrochlorothiazide may be of benefit in

treating chronic or recurrent cases.

- Increase the amount of green vegetables being fed to ensure adequate water intake and offer other nutritional support and vitamins (syringe feeding, tube feeding) if the patient is too weak to eat or will not eat.

Alternative and Complimentary Treatments[1,18,31,45]

- Dandelion leaf (Taraxacum officinale) - Increases diuresis and replaces potassium lost

- Goldenrod (Solidago spp.) - Generally strengthens weak kidneys

- Ginkgo (Ginkgo biloba) - Improves blood circulation of kidneys

- Cleavers Herb (Gallium aparine) - Improves lymph circulation, mild diuretic, reduces urinary tract inflammation

- Plantain (herb, not the fruit) – diuretic

- Boost Immune System
  ➢ Good nutrition
  ➢ Echinacea, Golden Seal, Systemajuv, Viarstem
  ➢ Decrease Stress – Bach Flower Homeopathic Remedy

- Tangerine peel and fruit – used for bladder health in Traditional Chinese medicine

- Probiotics- Lactobacillus, (such as Proviable) can be helpful in re-balancing the GI tract and provide anti-inflammatory support in rabbits.[48]

- No cranberry juice or cranberry products, as they are more likely to do harm than good in rabbits.[2]
  - ➤ The normal pH of rabbit urine is around eight.[2] (very alkaline). Cranberry therapy is used to acidify urine in humans and acidification of the urine of rabbits can lead to accumulation of another type of urinary calculi (sediment) called struvite.
  - ➤ The high sugar content of cranberry can also disrupt a rabbit's GI tract.

NEUROLOGIC DISEASES

Lead Poisoning

Rabbits love to chew on things, be it grass, foraging materials or artificial substances such as metal objects. Lead poisoning is fairly common and a serious concern for house rabbits both caged and allowed to "free roam" in the home or garden. As careful as owners may be, there may always be something hazardous that our rabbit friends can sink their teeth into.

Sources of lead in the home or garden include places like windowsills, old lead paint on furniture, toys, walls or baseboards, costume jewelry, solder on cage walls, galvanized cages and galvanized dishes.[44] Potential for lead poisoning is another reason to prevent rabbits from chewing on electrical cords, electrical appliances or computer cables, as the copper wire may contain lead.[44] Lead poisoning has some very non-specific clinical signs and the veterinary literature has not specifically defined a blood level threshold for lead poisoning. Blood lead levels less than 10 ug/dl are not considered diagnostic.[7,44] However, a recent study showed that non-specific clinical signs of lead poisoning, (anorexia and head tilt) were seen at levels of 3.4 ug/dl and 3.5 ug/dl, in the absence of concurrent disease. seizures were seen in patients with lead levels as low as 11.4 ug/dl. Bones are also an important reservoir for lead and high levels in the bone due to chronic accumulation may cause anemia while blood levels are low.[7] This information prompts us to consider the possibility of lead poisoning in rabbits that show non-specific signs, as it may be worthwhile to test them.[7,44] All rabbits that present with seizures should be tested for lead poisoning and rabbits that test positive for Encephalitozoon cuniculi should as well, since the clinical signs are so similar.[13]

Clinical Signs
- Neurologic
- ➢ Seizures, head tilt, falling to one side or favoring one side

- Non-specific
- ➢ Weight loss, lethargy, anorexia, abdominal pain, red urine, bloat and other signs of GI stasis

Diagnostics
- Complete blood count (CBC) – anemia, nucleated red blood cells

- Blood levels of lead

- Radiographs (skull, dental)

- MRI (Magnetic Resonance Imaging) / CT (Computed Tomography)

Differential Diagnoses
- Encephalitozoon cuniculi, pregnancy toxemia, ear infections, heat stroke, dental disease, etc.

Treatment

- Chelation therapy- binds to the lead in the body and aids to "flush it out" with Calcium EDTA

- Fluid therapy – prevents the kidneys from being overloaded with lead during the "flush out" treatment

- Post-treatment blood levels will determine if treatment should continue.

- Treatment typically is recommended for one to three weeks, depending on original blood levels.[44]

- Increase the amount of green vegetables being fed to ensure adequate water intake and offer other nutritional support and vitamins (syringe feeding, tube feeding) if the patient is too weak to eat or will not eat.

Alternative and Complimentary Treatments[1,18,31,45]

- Dandelion leaf (Taraxacum officinale) - Increases diuresis and replaces potassium lost during fluid therapy and diuresis

- Goldenrod (Solidago spp.) - Generally strengthens weak kidneys

- Ginkgo (Ginkgo biloba) - Improves blood circulation of kidneys

- Cleavers Herb (Gallium aparine) - Improves lymph circulation, mild diuretic, reduces urinary tract inflammation

- Plantain (herb, not the fruit) - diuretic

- Boost Immune System
➢ Good nutrition
➢ Echinacea, Golden Seal, Systemajuv, Viarstem
➢ Decrease Stress – Bach Flower Homeopathic Remedy

- Vitamin C

- Probiotics - Lactobacillus, (such as Proviable) can be helpful in re-balancing the GI tract and provide anti-inflammatory support in rabbits.[48]

- Homeopathics
➢ As an adjunct to standard medical treatment, per Heel, Inc.'s Routine Therapy. The Practitioner's Handbook of Homotoxicology[22]
➢ Reneel, Traumeel, Solidago compositum, Nux vomica, Thyreoidea composition, Coenzyme compositium, Ubichinon compositium

Encephalitozoon cuniculi

E. cuniculi is a strange microsporidian parasite that for many years was described in the literature as a protozoa but has recently been re-classified as fungi.[15,21] This microorganism is passed from rabbit to rabbit by urine-oral transmission and usually kits acquire it from their mothers.[12] It is then absorbed in the intestines and is carried to other organs by mononuclear cells. The "spores" of E. cuniculi prefer to accumulate and divide in kidney and brain tissue. About a month after infection, the spores in the kidney are excreted into the urine and spore shedding can continue for two to three months at a time. E. cuniculi can cause long-term kidney problems, especially in geriatric rabbits and the spores may be shed intermittently as a chronic, sub-clinical infection throughout the life of the rabbit.[3,5,12]

Clinical Signs

- Neurologic
- ➤ Seizures, head tilt, falling to one side or favoring one side

- Non-specific
- ➤ Weight loss, lethargy, anorexia, decreased appetite, bloat and other signs of GI stasis, dehydration, urinary incontinence

Diagnostics

- Radiographs (skull, dental)
- ➤ Not considered diagnostic, but will aid in ruling out other concurrent diseases.[44]

- MRI (Magnetic Resonance Imaging) / CT (Computed Tomography)
- ➤ Can be used to rule-out other, less common causes of neurological disease

- Blood antibody test (ELISA)

- Blood testing for lead

- Complete blood count (CBC), serum chemistry, electrolytes
- ➤ Azotemia – elevations in kidney values, signs of renal impairment[12]

Differential Diagnoses

- Lead poisoning, pregnancy toxemia, ear infections, heat stroke, dental disease, etc.

Treatment

- Oral benzimidazoles as directed
  - Fenbendazole, albendazole, oxybendazole are widely used[12,15]

- Fluid therapy – necessary if kidney function is impaired, aids to "flush out" toxins accumulated in the body.

- Increase the amount of green vegetables being fed to ensure adequate water intake and offer other nutritional support and vitamins (syringe feeding, tube feeding) if the patient is too weak to eat or will not eat.

Alternative and Complimentary Treatments[1,18,31,45]

- Homeopathy - Autonosode[35]

- Dandelion leaf (Taraxacum officinale) - Increases diuresis and replaces potassium lost during fluid therapy and diuresis

- Goldenrod (Solidago spp.) - Generally strengthens weak kidneys

- Ginkgo (Ginkgo biloba) - Improves blood circulation of kidneys

- Cleavers Herb (Gallium aparine) - Improves lymph circulation, mild diuretic, reduces urinary tract inflammation

- Plantain (herb, not the fruit) – diuretic

- Boost Immune System

> Good nutrition
> Echinacea, Golden Seal, Systemajuv, Viarstem
> Decrease Stress – Bach Flower Homeopathic Remedy

- Vitamin C

- Probiotics- Lactobacillus, (such as Proviable) can be helpful in re-balancing the GI tract and provide anti-inflammatory support in rabbits.[48]

Prevention
- Treatment of kits with fenbendazole[12]

RABIES

Although very rare in pet and house rabbits, all mammals can contract rabies. This disease is a major human health concern and it is important for owners to discuss with the. Rabies causes neurologic signs in rabbits and if presenting a rabbit to the veterinarian for neurologic symptoms, it is important to discuss the rabies vaccination status of other animals in the household or possible contact the rabbit could have had with wildlife. For example, pet rabbits allowed to free-roam in the garden unattended in North America can have encounters with raccoons or skunks, both common carriers of the rabies virus.

SENIOR DISEASES

As husbandry and preventative care are getting better for pet rabbits over time, our furry friends are living longer and happier lives. The typical lifespan of a rabbit can range from five to ten years and older. Rabbits have a relatively short lifespan and age more quickly than most people realize. Most rabbit experts and veterinarians consider rabbits to be geriatric at around four to five years of age or when degenerative disease changes begin.[5] As our beloved pets age, it is important to be aware of degenerative diseases and other disease processes that geriatric mammals, including rabbits, can develop. It is our duty to ensure that they live happy, comfortable lives until it is time to say goodbye. This section is intended as a general overview of what types of problems often arise in geriatric rabbits that owners need to be aware of.

Common Diseases and Problems of Geriatric Rabbits
Most disease processes in geriatric rabbits involve a certain level of pain. Methods of treating pain are then covered in more detail as related to the disease process.

These are a few things to look for in rabbits that may be exhibiting signs of pain:[9]

- Reluctance to move

- Decreased or absence of grooming

- Inappetence

- Closed eyes

- Hunched back

- Tense abdomen

- Hiding, anti-social when normally or previously social

- Teeth grinding

- Depression

- Aggression

- Dental disease

- Spondylosis
  - Spondylosis is a degenerative condition of the vertebrae and occurs most often in the lumbar spine. This disease basically stiffens the spine, making it less flexible and many older rabbits may develop an abnormal stance or have difficulty moving around, grooming, or consuming cecotrophs. Many rabbits appear to have weakened or painful musculature as well.[5]
  - Spondylosis can predispose rabbits to both arthritis and intervertebral disc degeneration.

- Osteoarthritis
  - This is the most common problem seen in geriatric mammals of all species. Over time, the cartilage that protects the joints breaks down and an inflammatory process takes over. Arthritis can be progressively more and more painful as the animal ages and causes a significant reduction in mobility.[5]

- Pododermatitis

- Uterine Cancer
  - Non-breeding females should be spayed at sexual maturity, or around three to six months of age. Breeding females should be spayed around three to four years of age in order to prevent uterine cancer as a senior rabbit.[5,6]

- Renal Disease and Encephalitozoon cuniculi
  - Older rabbits often suffer from renal damage sustained by chronic, subclinical infection with E. cuniculi.
  - More information can be found on E. cuniculi previously in this chapter.

Geriatric Rabbits and End of Life

Assessing quality of life by owners and veterinarians is extremely important in the geriatric patient. Making the decision to euthanize a beloved pet is never easy and sometimes it can be difficult to discuss when "it's time." Many veterinarians begin to introduce the "end of life" topic well before the expected death of a geriatric rabbit.[6] This way, owners, and veterinarians can be more prepared about making an informed decision before the situation gets even more stressful. The term euthanasia comes from Greek and means a "gentle and easy death." Euthanasia of any pet should be performed in a respectful, caring manner that minimizes stress on the patient and owner. Two phases of sedation and euthanasia technique are recommended, using first sedation or anesthesia prior to euthanasia.[5]

ZOONOTIC DISEASES

Many of these diseases are very rare in pet rabbits but are important for owners to be aware of. Others, like skin parasites, can be quite common.

Tularemia (Francisella tularensis) or "Rabbit Fever", Sylvatic Plague (Yersinia pestis), Mycobacteriosis (M. avium)[15] Campylobacter, Psoroptes spp., Dermatomycosis, Multiceps seralis, Taenia taeniaformis, Cheyletiella spp., Salmonella, Pasteurella multocida, Sarcoptes spp., bacterial infections from rabbit scratches and bites.[30]

CHAPTER 10: BREEDING

1.   Akawi, F. (2006, June 1). Snuffles in a Rabbit. Retrieved June 7, 2013 from Veterinary Information Network (VIN) Vet-to-Vet Alternative Medicine Message Board: www.vin.com

2.   Antinoff, N. (2010, July 11). Can Cranberry Products be Used for Urinary Tract Disease in Rabbits? Retrieved June 13, 2013 from Veterinary Information Network (VIN) Vet-to-Vet Mammals Small and Exotic Message Board: www.vin.com

3.   Antinoff, N. (2003). Urogenital Disorders of Ferrets and Rabbits. International Veterinary Emergency and Critical Care Symposium. Retrieved June 10, 2013 from Veterinary Information Network (VIN) website: www.vin.com

4.   Brown, S. (2012, January 13). Rabbits Need Exercise! Small Mammal Health Series. Veterinary Partner. Retrieved June 14, 2013 from Veterinary Partner website: www.veterinarypartner.com

5.   Carmel, B. (2010) The Elder Rabbit: Care and Welfare of the Geriatric Pet Rabbit. Australian Veterinary Association Proceedings. Retrieved June 12, 2013 from Veterinary Information Network (VIN) website: www.vin.com

6.   Carmel, B. (2009). The Healthy Rabbit. AAVAC-UEP. Retrieved June 14, 2013 from Veterinary Information Network (VIN) website: www.vin.com

7.   Carpenter, J. (2002). Common Neurological Diseases of Rabbits. Tufts Animal Expo. Retrieved June 10, 2013 from Veterinary Information Network (VIN) website: www.vin.com

8.   Dalton KP, Nicieza I, Balseiro A, Muguerza M, Rosell JM, Casais R, et al. (2012, November) Variant rabbit hemorrhagic disease virus in young rabbits, Spain. Emerg Infect Dis Abstract. Retrieved June 14, 2013 from Veterinary Information Network (VIN) website: www.vin.com

9.   Donnelly, T., Vella, D. (2009, June 29). Abnormal Behavior Problems and Recognition of Pain in Rabbits. Retrieved June 5, 2013 from Veterinary Information Network (VIN) website: www.vin.com

10.   Donnelly, T. Vella, D. (2009, April 28). Rabbit Behavior and Husbandry Relevant to Clinical Practice. Retrieved June 5, 2013 from Veterinary Information Network (VIN) website: www.vin.com

11.   Dunayer, E. (2011, May 3). Is Tea Tree Oil Toxic to Rabbits? Retrieved June 10, 2013 from Veterinary Information Network Vet-to-Vet Mammals Small and Exotic Message Board: www.vin.com

12.   Dutton, M. (2011) Diseases of the Urogenital of Exotic Compation Mammals I & III. ABVP. Retrieved June 10, 2013 from Veterinary Information Network (VIN) website: www.vin.com

13.   Fisher, G. (2011) Exotic Mammal Gastrointestinal Disease. Western

Veterinary Conference. Retrieved June 7, 2013 from Veterinary Information Network (VIN) website: www.vin.com

14.   Foil, C. (2001, August 21.) Flea Allergy Dermatitis. Retrieved June 7, 2013 from Veterinary Information Network (VIN) website: www.vin.com

15.   Garner, M. (2009). A Review of Common Diseases in Pet Rabbits. AAV. Retrieved June 10, 2013 from Veterinary Information Network (VIN) website: www.vin.com

16.   Glass, B. (2013, May). BunnyVac Pasteurella Vaccine. Retrieved June 15, 2013   from   Mad   Hatter   Rabbits   website: http://madhatterrabbits.files.wordpress.com/2013/05/bunnyvac-bob-glass-qa.pdf

17.   Gould, E. (2012, March). First Case of Rabbit Haemorrhagic Disease in Canada: Contaminated Flying Insect, vs. Long-term Infection Hypothesis. Mol Ecol.; 21(5): 1042-7. Retrieved June 13, 2013 from Veterinary Information Network (VIN) website: www.vin.com

18.   Griffith, D. (2010, June 24). Antivirals and Immunostimulants for Rabbits with Myxomatosis. . Retrieved June 17, 2013 from Veterinary Information Network (VIN) Vet-to-Vet Mammals Small and Exotic Message Board: www.vin.com

19.   Griffith, D. (2009, July 31). Dose of Vitamin B12 for Rabbits. Retrieved June 10, 2013 from Veterinary Information Network (VIN) Vet-to-Vet Alternative Medicine Message Board: www.vin.com

20.   Griffith, D. (2000, June 19). Rabbit Limb Paralysis/Bladder Atony. Retrieved June 15, 2013 from Veterinary Information Network (VIN) Vet-to-Vet Alternative Medicine Message Board: www.vin.com

21.   Harcourt-Brown, F. (2010) Diseases Related to Calcium Metabolism in Rabbits. World Small Animal Veterinary Association World Congress Proceedings. Retrieved June 11, 2013 from Veterinary Information Network (VIN) website: www.vin.com

22.   Heel, Inc. Routine Therapy. (2005).The Practitioner's Handbookof Homotoxicology.   Retrieved   June   17,   2013   from www.healingedge.net/pdf/heel_practitioners_handbook.pdf

23.   House Rabbit Society, Newkirk, M. (2013, January 16). Homeopathy: Alternative Medications for Rabbits. Retrieved June 9, 2013 from House Rabbit Society website: www.rabbit.org/homeopathy-alternative-medicines-for-rabbits/

24.   Iben, C., Kunzel, F., Handl, S. (2007) Clinical Nutrition in Small Animals (Guinea Pigs and Rabbits), GI Diseases. 17th ECVIM-CA Congress Proceedings. Retrieved June 10, 2013 from Veterinary Information Network (VIN) website: www.vin.com

25.   Iowa State University, Institute for International Cooperation in Animal Biologics, Center for Food Security and Public Health. (2008). Rabbit Hemorrhagic Disease. Retrieved June 12, 2013 from Veterinary Information Network (VIN) website: www.vin.com

26.   Ito, C. et al. (1979, April) Anti-inflammatory Actions of Proteases, Bromelain, Trypsin and their Mixed Preparation. Nippon Yakurigaku Zasshi. 75(3):227-37. Retrieved June 7, 2013 from Veterinary Information Network (VIN) website: www.vin.com

27.   Jaffe, P. (2013, April 23). Can Hyperbaric Oxygen Therapy be used for Rabbits? Retrieved June 10, 2013 from Veterinary Information Network (VIN) website: www.vin.com

28.   Jekl,   V.   (2012)   Rabbit   Behaviour   and   Welfare. WSAVA/FECAVA/BSAVA World Congress Proceedings. Retrieved June 7, 2013 from Veterinary Information Network (VIN) website: www.vin.com

29.   Jenkins, J. (2006). Conditions of the Feet of Rabbits and Rodents. British Small Animal Veterinary Congress. Retrieved from Veterinary Information Network (VIN) website: www.vin.com

30.   Johnson-Delaney, C. (1996). Exotic Companion Medicine Handbook for Veterinarians. Rabbits, 1-12.

31.   Jones, P. (2011, January 5). Shepherd's Purse for Urinary Sludge in Rabbit: Diet Therapy and Herbals for Urinary Sludge in Rabbits. Retrieved June 7, 2013 from Veterinary Information Network (VIN) website: www.vin.com

32.   Kohles, M. (2010) Gastrointestinal Function and Proper Nutrition of the Rabbit. AAVAC-UEP Conference Proceedings. Retrieved June 9, 2013 from Veterinary Information Network (VIN) website: www.vin.com

33.   Lee, D. et al. (2000). Evaluation of Probiotic Treatment in Neonatal Animal Model. Pediatr Surg Int. 16(4): 237-42. Retrieved June 6, 2013 from Veterinary Information Network (VIN) website: www.vin.com

34.   Lennox, A. (2006). Dentistry of Rabbits. Western Veterinary Conference Proceedings. Retrieved June 10, 2013 from Veterinary Information Network (VIN) website: www.vin.com

35.   Limehouse,   J.   (2007,   May   12).   Autonosode   Treatment   for Encephalitozoon Infection in a Rabbit. Retrieved June 16, 2013 from Veterinary Information Network (VIN) Vet-to-Vet Alternative Medicine Message Board: www.vin.com

36.   Longsheng, Y. et al. (2008, August). Compound Chinese Herbal Medicinal Ingredients Can Enhance Immune Response and Efficacy of RHD Vaccine in Rabbit. Vaccine. 26(35): 4451-5. Retrieved June 7, 2013 from Veterinary Information Network (VIN): www.vin.com

37.   Mayer, J. (2011). Small Mammal Dermatology: Dermatologic Diseases of ECM I, II & III. ABVP. Retrieved June 9, 2013 from Veterinary Information Network (VIN) website: www.vin.com

38.   Meredith, A. (2008). Dermatological Conditions of Rodents and Rabbits. World Small Animal Veterinary Association World Congress Proceedings. Retrieved June 7, 2013 from Veterinary Information Network (VIN) website: www.vin.com

39.   Murray, M. (2002). Rabbit Gastroenterology. Western Veterinary Conference Proceedings. Retrieved June 9, 2013 from Veterinary Information Network (VIN) website: www.vin.com

40.   Palmquist, R. (2009, November 25). Discontinue NSAID Therapy Prior to Beginning Homeopathy. Retrieved June 17, 2013 from Veterinary Information Network (VIN) Vet-to-Vet Alternative Medicine Message Board: www.vin.com

41.   Palmquist, R. (2011, July 6). Discussion on Milk Thistle and Zeel. Retrieved June 12, 2013 from Veterinary Information Network (VIN) Vet-to-Vet Alternative Medicine Message Board: www.vin.com

42.   Porter, S. (2008). Common Disorders in Rodents and Rabbits. Atlantic Coast Veterinary Conference. Retrieved June 8, 2013 from Veterinary Information Network (VIN) website: www.vin.com

43.   Rhody, J. (2012). What's Up Doc? Rabbit Medicine 101. Western Veterinary Conference. Retrieved June 14, 2013 from Veterinary Information Network (VIN) website: www.vin.com

44.   Rosenwax, A. (2009) Lead Exposure in Pet Rabbits.   AAVAC-UEP. Retrieved June 15, 2013 from Veterinary Information Network (VIN) website: www.vin.com

45.   Tilford, G. (2004). Therapeutic Uses of Herbs. Western Veterinary Conference. Retrieved on June 10, 2013 from Veterinary Information Network (VIN) website: www.vin.com

46.   Vithoulkas, G. (n.d.) Apis mellifica. Retrieved June 16, 2013 from the International   Academy   of   Classical   Homeopathy   website: http://www.vithoulkas.com/en/books-study/2097.html

47.   Weese, S. (2011, May 13). Rabbit Hemorrhagic Disease (RHD) Diagnosed in Pet Rabbit from Canada. Retrieved June 13, 2013 from Veterinary Information Network (VIN) Vet-to-Vet Mammals Small and Exotic Message Board: www.vin.com

48.   Zorgniotti, F. (2011, June 15). Use of Proviable-RB Probiotic in Rabbits. Retrieved June 10, 2013 from Veterinary Information Network (VIN) Vet-to-Vet Mammals Small and Exotic Message Board: www.vin.com

CHAPTER 10
BREEDING

Many pet rabbit owners become involved in pedigree showing and may want to start a breeding program as a hobby or business at home. This is a brief outline to guide those interested in breeding and reproduction. Breeding behaviors, gestation (pregnancy), technique and difficulties will be discussed.

Young does reach sexual maturity and are able to breed at around six months of age.[4] This age may be slightly older (eight to nine months) for giant breeds. Bucks can start breeding a little earlier than their female counterparts, at roughly four to seven months of age. It is recommended that young bucks be limited to two matings per month and then the number gradually increased. In a colony of rabbits, one buck can "service" about ten does.

This is commonly done in laboratory or commercial settings, and bucks will breed on average one doe per week.[4]

Keeping everyone separated for twenty-one to thirty days before breeding will decrease the chances of false pregnancy and fighting. More information about false pregnancies is outlined in the Spay and Neuter chapter. Female rabbits and other lagomorphs do not have reproductive cycles like most other mammals. Estrus behavior, or "heat" may be seen even though the actual estrous cycle does not occur. Rabbits are induced or spontaneous ovulators, meaning that first, the male must mate with the female before ovulation begins. Ovulation occurs approximately ten hours after copulation. Other induced ovulators include the cat and ferret.[2]

Even though does must be mated before ovulation will occur, they do have a certain rhythm of sexual receptivity, usually every four to six days.[2] They are typically sexually receptive to the male several hours before the time of ovulation.[2] It is best to take the doe to the buck's cage or housing area for mating.[4] Then the "mating chase" begins. Courtship can appear as fast, aggressive chasing between rabbits. However, courtship chasing can be distinguished in that when the pursued rabbit is caught, it is not attacked.

Once the female is "caught" in the pursuit, courtship continues when the male raises up his haunches and "flags" his tail to her while walking with a stiff-legged gait.[2] He repeats this action for three or four times in succession, sometimes circling her. Many times tail flagging is combined with epuresis. Epuresis or enurination is when the male rabbit emits a stream of urine at the female during the courtship display.[2] Circling the female is very often involved in this process, but it is most common for the buck to run in front of the doe and twist his hindquarters at her while emitting the urine jet. Epuresis can sometimes be a sign of aggression, and this is often seen when the doe enurinates a buck that is pestering her.[2] Epuresis is also used between bucks, such as when an older, more dominant buck is trying to drive off a younger one.[2]

Females in estrus are hyperactive and will react or "flinch" their back when touched. A characteristic sign of estrus in the rabbit is lordosis – the reverse bending and flattening of the back, thus raising the pelvis in presentation for the male to mount. Females will have an enlarged, red-purple vulva at the time of receptivity.[2] The most reliable indicator of estrus is the visualization of lordosis, and vaginal smears are not helpful in determining when to breed.[2]

After the buck "services" the doe, he will fall over on his back or on his side. Many breeders recommend re-mating the pair the same day, about five hours later.[4]

Gestation (pregnancy) length in rabbits is approximately thirty to thirty-three days.[1,2] Large breeds can produce up to eight to twelve kits per litter and small breeds four to five kits per litter.[2] Rabbits lactate during gestation and sexual desire decreases significantly while kits are nursing.[2] It is possible for does to have five litters a year but this is generally not recommended. If a litter is lost at birth, the doe should be receptive to breeding again (estrus) three to four days later.[4]

Pregnancy is best detected by palpation. Owners can have an experienced rabbit breeder come and check the doe about ten days after breeding when the amniotic sacs around the developing kits are about the size of blueberries. At about two weeks after breeding, they are the size of olives or large marbles. It is not terribly hard to learn palpation but it takes lots of practice. Place your doe on a flat surface and secure her head gently. Using the other hand, gently feel into the abdomen just in front of the pelvis, in a motion like you are giving her belly a deep massage. It may be worthwhile to have an experienced breeder teach you what to feel for and often they can direct you if you are palpating too close to the chest.

Sometimes rabbits don't "breed like rabbits" and difficulties can occur. Failure to get pregnant often is due to the doe being too old, too overweight, or has a secondary disease process that reduces fertility. If a doe has not become pregnant after several attempts, don't get discouraged! It is worthwhile to contact a rabbit-savvy veterinarian or seasoned rabbit breeder and they can help you and your doe.

1.   Donnelly, T., Vella, D. (2009, June 9). Rabbit Anatomy and Physiology Relevant to Clinical Practice. Retrieved June 5, 2013 from Veterinary Information Network (VIN) website: www.vin.com

2.   Donnelly, T. Vella, D. (2009, April 28). Rabbit Behavior and Husbandry Relevant to Clinical Practice. Retrieved June 5, 2013 from Veterinary Information Network (VIN) website: www.vin.com

3.   Gill, C. Sept/Oct 2004. The Art of Palpation. Countryside Magazine. Retrieved   June   14,   2013   from   ARBA   website: https://www.arba.net/PDFs/palpation.pdf

4.   Proverbs, G., Quintyne, R. (1992, April). CARDI Factsheet: A Guide to Breeding   Rabbits.   Retrieved   June   14,   2013   from http://www.fao.org/docs/eims/upload/agrotech/1939/04-80.pdf

CHAPTER 11
EXHIBITIONS AND SHOWS

Rabbit shows and exhibitions are wonderful, social events where rabbit enthusiasts can gather, show excellent specimens, learn, and have a good time. There are hundreds of rabbit shows and exhibitions every year in many different countries. There are options for every experience level, from children to seasoned experts and every rabbit can have the opportunity to "show off."

The main organizations promoting rabbit shows and exhibitions in English-speaking countries are the American Rabbit Breeder's Association (ARBA), the House Rabbit Society, the British Rabbit Council, 4-H, and FFA. The American Rabbit Breeder's Association has over 23,000 members in the US, Canada, and abroad.[2] Conventions and shows are held on a regular basis at the local club, State or Provence, and National levels. ARBA has many different types of variety and breed classes, including junior and pre-junior, meat, fur and wool and youth.[2] Points are given at shows based on the ARBA Standard of Perfection for each recognized breed category.[2] All animals must be permanently and legibly tattooed in the left ear in order to be shown in a breed or pedigree class.[2] Winners from initial classes go on to compete with one another for best of breed, best of sex, best overall, etc.

Many classes are also offered at shows for pet (non-pedigreed) rabbits. 4-H and FFA (Future Farmers of America) also offer a great opportunity for youth to learn about rabbits and showmanship. These shows focus more on showmanship rather than their pet's breed perfection, and knowledge is always of utmost importance. Youth are encouraged to know as much about the breeds as possible and to seek out information (such as 4-H books, handouts, the ARBA Standard of Perfection, Better Guide to Raising Rabbits and Cavies, etc.).[1] The judges at these types of youth shows judge not only the rabbit, but pay close attention to how the animal is "shown." For example, if the judge asks for the teeth to be "checked," then the competitor should look themselves. If the judge then asks for the teeth to be "shown," then the judge wants to see them.[1]

Shows teach children and youth the importance of good husbandry, grooming and instills proper, safe handling techniques. Competitors are expected to groom themselves and their rabbits well, to speak loudly and clearly, smile, and to help your neighbor if the judge asks that the competitors "switch rabbits." A youth may be able to win the competition by fixing or improving the presentation or posing of their neighbor's entry.[1]

The British Rabbit Society (BRC) also sponsors hundreds of shows a year at local, Regional and National levels.[3] These shows include classes based on breed, sex and age. Many offer pet classes as well as pedigree classes. In order to be eligible to show in a pedigree class at a BRC show, each entry must be "rung" or have a registered metal ring around its foot and the owner must be a member of the BRC.[7] These metal rings are distributed to breeders by the BRC. Points are awarded to each entry for individual attributes as determined by the BRC Breed Standard. Winners from initial classes go on to compete with one another for best of breed, best of sex, best overall, etc. BRC shows are rated from low (1) to high (5) based on the amounts of awards given at each show.[3]

Rabbit Expositions or Expos are great social events for owners and rabbits alike. Many of these Expos are more like a fair than a competitive venue. Many Expos feature competitions but their main focus is on education, outreach, socialization and fun. Purveyors of rabbit products, breeders, and veterinarians are usually on hand promoting products and educational materials. National rabbit welfare and rescue groups such as the House Rabbit Society, RSPCA or State Rabbit Breeder's Associations often sponsor these types of events. Many venues encourage owners to bring their rabbits to the Expo to join in on the fun. Rabbit Stations and "bunny photography" booths are available for rabbits to relax and munch hay while their owners shop and socialize.6

POSING RABBITS FOR SHOW

All five (ARBA recognized) body types are posed in the same manner. The front feet must always be in line with the eye and the back feet must be in line with the hock (stifle).[4] Many other groups, like 4-H and the BRC also encourage similar rabbit posing techniques. Be sure to pose the rabbit lying down and pose them the same way each time. The curve of the back should be relaxed but not so in that the rabbit appears "stretched out." Bunching a rabbit up too much can cover up faults but too much can hurt an exceptionally good-looking breed or type specimen.[4] The key to successfully posing is to practice, practice, and practice keeping the rabbit calm and rewarding him throughout the process.

ENTERING A RABBIT SHOW

In order to enter a rabbit show, contact a local rabbit breeders association or national group. Most require that owners be a member of the organization in order to enter the rabbits into competition. Many shows are advertised online and entry forms and information are easily obtained. Return the entry form with the appropriate fees for the classes you wish to enter.[6,7] Be sure that your rabbit has the appropriate tattoo or foot ring before entering in a pedigree class. At the show, you will be assigned a pen number and checked in.[7] Settle your rabbit in with fresh hay, water and food as quickly as possible. When the judging begins, you may not be allowed to handle your rabbit. At most shows, especially in the UK, club stewards will retrieve your rabbit for showing and take it to the judging table. Local clubs, pet classes, and youth (4-H, FFA) shows allow the owners to handle the rabbits during judging and many encourage it. Keep in mind if you are showing in a pet class, as they are judged on tameness, good health, and cleanliness rather than breed standard.[7] While it is exciting to win at a show, it is most important for you and your rabbit to have a fun, relaxing outing together.

RABBIT SHOW JUMPING

Rabbit show jumping is a little bit like equestrian show jumping or agility for dogs. This activity began in Sweden in the 1970s and has taken the world by storm. Shows featuring show jumping can be found through 4-H shows, county and state fairs and organizations such as the American Association of Sporting Events for Rabbits. Rabbits with long legs and long backs are preferred for jumping sports. Lops may injure themselves tumbling over their long floppy ears and Angora breeds may have difficulty seeing the obstacles unless their facial hair is cut short.[8] Competing rabbits are trained and prompted to jump over obstacles of differing heights. One should always have their rabbit master lower obstacles before advancing to taller ones, lessening the risk of injury.

CHAPTER 11: EXHIBITIONS AND SHOWS

1.   4-H Showmanship. (n.d.). American Rabbit Breeder's Association Articles.   Retrieved   on   June   13,   2013   from: https://www.arba.net/PDFs/4HShowmanship.pdf

2.   American Rabbit Breeder's Association. (2013, January 1). Official Show Rules   of   the   ARBA.   Retrieved   on   June   13,   2013   from: https://www.arba.net/PDFs/show_rules.pdf

3.   British Rabbit Council. (n.d.) Official Website. Retrieved on June 14, 2013 from: http://www.thebrc.org

4.   Ekstrom, J. (n.d.) Posing. Retrieved on June 14, 2013 from American Rabbit Breeder's Association website: https://www.arba.net/PDFs/posing.pdf

5.   Michigan State Rabbit Breeder's Association. (n.d.) Official Website. Retrieved on June 14, 2013 from: http://www.msrba.net/

6.   Missouri HRS Bunny Expo. (2013). Online Promotional Brochure. Retrieved on June 15, 2013 from: http://www.hrsmostl.org/Bunny-Expo-2011.html

7.   Rabbit Shows. (n.d.) A Day at a Rabbit Show. Retrieved on June 14, 2013 from: http://www.rabbit-shows.co.uk/what-goes-on-at-a-rabbit-show/

8.   Rabbit Show Jumping. (2013, May 12). Retrieved on June 15, 2013 from Wikipedia:
http://en.wikipedia.org/wiki/American_Association_of_Sporting_Events_for_Rabbits

RESOURCES

Nutritional, Health, Medical Information Resources
Oxbow Animal Health offers high-quality grasses, feeds, bedding and nutrition products for rabbits and other small mammals in North America and abroad. They also offer free educational materials through their website. Many of their products can be found online and in pet stores.
www.oxbowanimalhealth.com

Doctors Foster and Smith is an online supplier of health, nutrition, and veterinary products for many species of animals in North America.
www.drsfostersmith.com

The Original Bach Flower Rescue Remedy Pets is a great, alcohol-free homeopathic treatment balancing the mind and body.
www.bachflower.com/alcohol-free-bach-flower-remedies

Heel, Inc. offers homeopathic remedies such as Taumeel) and educational materials worldwide through its website.
www.heelusa.com

Heel, Inc.'s Practitioner's Handbook of Homotoxoicology is available for free download through:
www.healingedge.net/pdf/heel_practitioners_handbook.pdf

Rabbit Welfare Association and Fund has a list of excellent fruit, vegetable and herbs that boost rabbits' health:
www.rabbitwelfare.co.uk/resources/content/info-sheets/safefoods.htm

House Rabbit Online Community, blog, toys, play houses, organics and nutritional products:

www.binkybunny.com

KW Cages Advanced Design website and catalog has a tremendous amount of options for housing, cages, enrichment, nutrition, etc. for house rabbit owners and commercial rabbit producers.
www.kwcages.com

Veterinary Partner is veterinary peer-reviewed, reliable free online resource for pet owners wanting to learn about the health and husbandry of any species.
www.veterinarypartner.com

DebMark Rabbit Education Resource is an online recommended reading list for rabbit enthusiasts wanting to expand their general knowledge of rabbits, husbandry, and health.
www.debmark.com/rabbits/books.htm

The House Rabbit Society has an extensive list of articles written by experts available for free online on any topic of interest, ranging from welfare to breeding to alternative medical treatments.
www.rabbit.org/category/health/

Most rabbit enthusiast and welfare groups have extensive online article databases on their websites for reliable rabbit information and advice.

Rabbit-friendly Veterinarians
Association of Exotic Mammal Veterinarians, veterinarian listings for the US, Canada and abroad:
www.aemv.org

Exotic Pet Vet. Net, educational resource with veterinary listings:
www.exoticpetvet.net

House Rabbit Society's Veterinary Listings for the US, Canada and abroad:
www.rabbit.org/vet-listings

Rabbit Vets UK listings and database for UK rabbit-friendly veterinarians.
www.rabbit-vet.co.uk

Breeders' Associations and Rescue Groups
American Rabbit Breeders Association (ARBA) offers educational materials, welfare recommendations and guidelines, show schedules, local club information in the US, Canada and abroad through its website.
www.arba.net

The British Rabbit Council (BRC) offers educational materials, welfare recommendations and guidelines, show schedules, local club information in the UK, shopping, etc. through its website.
www.thebrc.org

House Rabbit Society offers educational materials, welfare recommendations and guidelines, information on local chapters, Expos, rescued rabbit database, foster and adoption programs, throughout the US, Canada and abroad.
www.rabbit.org

The Royal Society for the Prevention of Cruelty to Animals is an animal rights and welfare group in the UK that promotes educational materials, adoption and foster programs for all species of animals.
www.rspca.org.uk
In Australia, Canada, and other Commonwealth countries:
www.rspca.org.au
www.animalrightszone.com/canada/rspca/

Rabbit Breeders Canada is a rabbit breeders' directory and enthusiasts group that provides educational resources, breeder, local chapter, rabbit supplies and show information.
www.rabbitbreeders.ca

The Humane Society International is an animal rights and welfare organization promoting the well-being of all animals. Links to local groups, adoptions, and other educational materials can be found on their international website.
www.hsi.or

Made in the USA
Middletown, DE
26 June 2017